The Church's Ultimate Goal

Developing Your Corporate Destiny

Don Meares

Albury Press
2448 East Lewis Street, Suite 4700
Tulsa, Oklahoma 74137

Unless otherwise indicated, all scripture quotations are taken from the *King James Version* of the Bible.

Scripture quotations marked NASB are taken from the *New American Standard Bible*, copyright © 1960, 1962, 1963, 1968, 1971, 1973, 1975, 1977 by the Lockman Foundation. Used by permission.

Scripture quotations marked RSV are taken from the *Revised Standard Version of the Bible*, copyright © 1946, Old Testament section copyright © 1952 by the Division of Christian Education of the Churches of Christ in the United States of America and is used by permission.

The Church's Ultimate Goal
Developing Your Corporate Destiny
ISBN 1-88008-926-2
Copyright by Don Meares

Published by Albury Press
2448 East Lewis Street, Suite 4700
Tulsa, Oklahoma 74137

Printed in the United States of America.
All rights reserved under International Copyright Law.
Contents and / or cover may not be reproduced in whole or in part in any form without the express written consent of the Publisher.

Acknowledgments

I am extremely grateful for the godly heritage that I have in the Lord. As the middle child of a pastor with an apostolic calling, I grew up with an enormous amount of exposure to men and women of God. Sometimes I feel like I have "seen it all" when it comes to the things of God and the people of God. I have been influenced by many people during my lifetime, but none have touched me to the degree that my parents have.

My deepest appreciation goes to Dad — Bishop John Meares — and Mother — Elder Mary Lee Meares. I dedicate this book to them.

Contents

Foreword

When God joins people together, it is a supernatural act. During the past ten years I have been keenly aware that such a joining has occurred between Don Meares and me. There is a covenant friendship we have that only God could have orchestrated.

I had a strong denominational upbringing, so I know how most churches operate. The first time I spoke at Evangel Church, where Don pastors, I realized there was something different about this local church. Over the years, as I have gotten to know Don and Evangel Church better, I know that the difference is biblical government. They have an apostolic foundation. They have a senior pastor who is honored as the mouthpiece of God. They have elders and deacons who are servants in the truest, biblical sense.

The apostolic mantle on Don's dad, Bishop John Meares, has also touched my life. It was he who encouraged me, as a traveling minister, to put down roots as a senior pastor of a local church. I am grateful for his godly wisdom.

I highly recommend this book to every local church leader. It will make a difference in your church!

—Luther Blackwell

Introduction

I believe that everything in the Bible is true—every pattern, every principle, every promise. I also believe, however, that unless I can integrate those truths into my lifestyle and into the workings of my local church, they are of little value to me.

The information included in the six chapters of this book is not theory. The principles are all found in the Word of God and, by the grace of God, they have been borne out in my own personal experience—often through trial and error, sometimes through great pain.

As I wrote this book, I often directed my statements to pastors and church leaders, but everyone who is planted in a local church family can benefit from the truths I have shared. Some of the things you will read may surprise you, especially if you have been brought up in a denomination that teaches congregational rule. I pray that you will open your heart as you read and allow the Holy Spirit to speak to you. Individual destiny, corporate destiny, scriptural joining, corporate unity, corporate prayer and servanthood—these are issues which will change the way you think and the way you act in the life of your local church.

—Don Meares

1

Individual Destiny

The harsh sound of the siren blares in his ears as the ambulance swiftly weaves in and out of the heavy, evening traffic. "Boston General, this is Unit 182. How do you copy?"

"We've got ya, 182," the E.R. attendant responds. "Go ahead."

"Boston General, we've got a 55-year-old male who called in complaining of severe chest pains. By the time we arrived, he was in fibrillation and is now in full arrest. CPR is in progress."

"Roger, 182. We'll be ready for you."

In a haze, the man tries to make sense out of what's happening to him. Where are the grandkids? Only moments before they had been playing together.

Suddenly the movement of the ambulance comes to an abrupt stop as doors are jerked open and the stretcher he's on is quickly lifted out.

"Coming through," they shout. "Code Blue!"

"Get him in trauma one. Hook up the monitor — continue pumping his chest and start bagging him," the emergency room doctor orders.

Suspended near the ceiling, above his own body, the man looks with amazement to the activity below. "What's happening to me!?" The scream, though silent, is real, but only his ears can hear it.

"Do we have a rhythm?" asks the doctor. "Not yet," responds the nurse. Muttering to himself, the doctor says, "Shock at 200 joules — Clear!" The body jumps, but no life responds.

"Give him an amp of epinephrine and set at 300. Clear!" The process continues with more medication and shocks feverishly administered while the pumping and bagging become so intense sweat pours profusely off the brows of the therapists.

"He's gone. We've lost him," are the final words he hears as the view from the ceiling fades into an entirely different setting.

Whether from reality or memory, he's not sure, the words come to him, "To be absent from the body is to be present with the Lord."

"Heaven. I'm standing in heaven!" The realization is so staggering that even in the afterlife of eternity he is taken back by the one hope to which he had clung all these years.

"I'm really here," he marvels. "It worked! All those years of going to church, reading the Bible and doing good deeds really worked. I wonder what happens now?"

Before he can think that question through, however, he hears his name being called and is instantly before a great, white throne surrounded by an awesome golden hue. The throne of Almighty God.

"No problem," he reasons. "I believe in Jesus and besides, I lived a really good life. I taught Sunday School, served on the deacon board and even shared Christ with folks at work." This should be the proverbial "piece of cake."

"Is his name in the book?" the question comes from nowhere and everywhere simultaneously. "I do not find it here, Lord," answers the keeper of records.

"But, that's impossible," he mumbles, overcome by the revelation of the scribe. "It has to be in there. I've been in the church for over fifty years. I've raised my children to respect the church and its teachings, and even my grandchildren love to go to church with me. This must be some terrible mistake."

"Depart from Me, you that work iniquity." A cold shiver consumes the man that trusted on the arm of the flesh rather than the direction of the Spirit of the Lord. "NO!" he screams as he feels everything around him begin to change from peace into eternal torment. "NO, NO, NO! This can't be happening. I joined the church. I called Jesus, Lord. How could I have been so misguided? How?"

And then he awakes. A dream. It had only been a dream, but my God, what a nightmare. Could this possibly be his destiny?

Destiny. Everyone on this planet has one and yet many never fulfill, or even discover, their God-given destiny. Like the man in the previous story, they think that they have their "act together" only to discover, when it is too late, that they don't even have all the proper pieces to the puzzle. That which they believed to have been His will turns out to be nothing more than a humanistic attempt to satisfy a religious whim of "doing it for God."

What is your destiny in God? By that, I mean, what are you here for? What is it that God has for you to do with your life that will totally fulfill you and accomplish for Him what He intends for your life to accomplish? What is your vision?

The Bible declares that **where there is no vision, the people perish...** (Proverbs 29:18). Other translations of this scripture say that people with no vision are "unrestrained" or "running wild." The Hebrew word, para, translated "perish" in this verse, literally means "naked." That's right. Without vision from God, you and I are literally walking around this planet without the proper attire for life. Far more important than clothes, vision enables us to be covered with His blessing and anointing so that all we do will prosper and remain.

So, I'll ask you the question again. What is it that God has destined for your life? What are you here for?

Part of our problem in answering these questions is the erroneous teaching that we have been given concerning what it really means to be a Christian. The gospel has been so "watered down" in some instances that all we know of serving Jesus is that to be saved will allow us to "miss hell and go to heaven."

If that's all you know about serving Jesus, then you don't know much at all. In fact, Jesus' primary concern for you is not whether you make heaven and miss hell, but rather that you discover your God-given destiny and fulfill His purpose in and through your earthly life.

I can hear many of you now. "Wait a minute, preacher! Jesus' total mission on this earth was to rescue us from hell and take us to heaven." Wrong, wrong, wrong! Jesus' mission was to rescue us from darkness and translate us into light.

> **Again therefore Jesus spoke to them, saying, "I am the light of the world; he who follows Me shall not walk in the darkness, but shall have the light of life."**
> **John 8:12 NASB**

Peter's first epistle states it this way: **But ye are a chosen generation, a royal priesthood, an holy nation, a peculiar people; that ye should shew forth the praises of him who hath called you out of darkness into his marvellous light.**

That's the only reason that we can discover our destiny in God. It is as we "walk in the light as He is in the light" that we see as He sees and hear as He hears. According to Isaiah, it is imperative to see and hear as God does.

> **For as the heavens are higher than the earth, so are my ways higher than your ways, and my thoughts than your thoughts.**
>
> **Isaiah 55:9**

You see, God doesn't think like you and I do. We deal with a finite life cycle and finite things within that life cycle. God deals with eternity. Everything in God is infinite and a part of His total plan for all the eons. Solomon in writing Ecclesiastes understood this when he wrote,

> **He has made everything appropriate in its time. He has also set eternity in their heart, yet so that man will not find out the work which God has done from the beginning even to the end.**
>
> **Ecclesiastes 3:11 NASB**

You may be thinking, "Well fine, but what has that got to do with me?" The answer to that, my brother and sister, is — EVERYTHING! You and I are not here just to "make heaven and miss hell," we are here to fulfill His destiny and vision for our lives. And, everything that He has destined us to do has eternal value in the kingdom of God. Do you understand what I just stated? You and I are a part of the eternal purpose of God and His kingdom. We are important!

"Oh, yeah?" you may be thinking. "Well, if I'm so important, why are things so hard? It seems the more that I try to accomplish for God, the more problems I encounter. Not just concerning spiritual things either. Every day is filled with more and more problems. Why is life so tough if I'm so important?"

A portion of the answer to these questions may be found in one of the questions themselves. Are you attempting to accomplish His destiny for your life based on the revelation He has given you, or are you attempting to make the things you have chosen to do become His destiny by your own human effort?

God's vision for your life can only come from Him. Without His vision you will never accomplish your destiny.

Good ideas are never enough. It's not a matter of, "Here, Lord. I give all this stuff to You for Your glory." Oh, no! God's not going to take all our "junk" and then give it back with His blessing. He is going to receive what we give Him and then return to us His divine will and purpose for our lives which may or may not include the things that we have done to date. That's why we must "walk in the light." It's only in learning of Him that we are able to be conformed to His likeness. Whether you like this statement or not, it's still true. Unless you and I discover and walk in God's divine destiny for our lives, then all our works count for nothing. Consider the following:

> For no man can lay a foundation other than the one which is laid, which is Jesus Christ.
>
> Now if any man builds upon the foundation with gold, silver, precious stones, wood, hay, straw,
>
> Each man's work will become evident; for the day will show it, because it is to be revealed with fire; and the fire itself will test the quality of each man's work.
>
> If any man's work which he has built upon it remains, he shall receive a reward.
>
> If any man's work is burned up, he shall suffer loss; but he himself shall be saved, yet so as through fire.
>
> **1 Corinthians 3:11-15** NASB

You may not be ready for what I'm about to tell you, but nonetheless you must understand the following. When you and I stand before Almighty God on the day of judgment, all of our works are going to be judged and only what isn't consumed by His fire will merit us anything! That's right. ALL our works are going to be judged, and rewards in heaven will be given based on whether those works were a part of His destiny for our lives of just self-righteous acts that we did on our own. Are you ready for Judgment Day?

"Well, of course I am," you may be thinking; but are you really prepared for Judgment Day? "Well, I've accepted

Jesus Christ as my Savior and I've joined a local church. I believe that I was lost and undone without Christ and that His shed blood alone washes away my sin and allows me to have right standing with God. Doesn't that make me ready for Judgment Day?" NO, IT DOESN'T! The born-again experience brings you back into fellowship with God and restores your relationship with the Father, but only embracing Jesus as Lord of your life prepares you for an eternity with Him in heaven. The issue here isn't "relationship" but rather "lordship."

Consider these words from the gospel of Matthew when Jesus told the people:

> **So then, you will know them by their fruits.**
> **Not every one who says to me, "Lord, Lord," will enter the kingdom of heaven; but he who does the will of My Father who is in heaven.**
>
> Matthew 7:20-21 NASB

What a shock! Here is a person who obviously believes he is prepared for heaven because he *called* Jesus, Lord. *Calling* Him Lord, however, and His actually *being* Lord are two entirely different things.

What does it mean for Jesus to be Lord? Many teach that the very fact we are saved insures us He is our Lord. Ponder with me for a moment, however, the family unit to which you belong. I'm speaking of your natural family — Mom, Dad, brothers, sisters and so forth. Is it possible to be "born in the family" and yet be so rebellious or self-centered that you do not reap the benefits of family living? Of course it is. Many of us can immediately identify individuals within our families who just don't seem to understand how to live responsibly as a family member. Most of these members find themselves at odds with the instructions and directions given by the father of the family. They are determined to do things "their way" and prove to everyone else that their way is the right way. Invariably these misguided individuals end up losing everything, including the privileges that should have been theirs for being in the family.

So it is in the body of Christ. Many today call Him Lord but never seek Him as to His direction, purpose and destiny for their lives. Instead, they assume He will bless whatever they do as long as they say they are doing it "for the glory of God." HOGWASH! Where do you and I get the idea that we know what's best for our lives? My God, we were totally screwed up before Jesus came into our lives, and now we are going to tell Him how we are to live? I think not! Lordship demands that we submit ourselves unto the only One Who knows why we are here and what we are supposed to accomplish during our time on this earth.

"Now, wait just a minute," you may be thinking. "You don't have any idea what I've done for Christ. Why, man, I've seen some real miracles in my time. Yes, sir. I'm talking about real miracles. Healing, deliverance and things like that. I guarantee you that God is pleased with what I'm doing." Really? Well, let's look a little further in Matthew's writing.

> Many will say to Me on that day, "Lord, Lord, did we not prophesy in Your name, and in Your name cast out demons, and in Your name perform many miracles?"
> And then I will declare to them, "I never knew you; Depart from Me, you who practice lawlessness."
> Matthew 7:22-23 NASB

WHAT? You mean none of that stuff counts? Oh, it counts all right. It counts against you unless you did it under His lordship. Notice that the scripture says "many" will say on that day — not a few, but "many." That tells me a whole lot of people are going to be thoroughly shaken on Judgment Day when they stand before a sovereign God to have their works from this life judged by His fire.

Judgment Day. There are those distasteful words again. Most Christians, when they hear anyone begin to speak on judgment, immediately shut down because "we're under grace, brother, not judgment." Excuse me, but whether you like it or not, there is coming a day of eternal judgment when all that we have done will be placed in the fire of His glory, and only what we did under His lordship will count. According to scripture, eternal judgment is one of the elementary principles of every believer's life.

> **Therefore leaving the elementary teaching about the Christ, let us press on to maturity, not laying again a foundation of repentance from dead works and of faith toward God,**
>
> **Of instruction about washings, and laying on of hands, and the resurrection of the dead, and eternal judgment.**
>
> **Hebrews 6:1-2 NASB**

As Sherlock Holmes would say, "Elementary, my dear Christian!" So, why don't we hear more teaching on eternal judgment? Why doesn't somebody tell us the truth?

I can answer that. Because if the truth were really preached, we'd lose about half our church members! They couldn't take it. Why? Because in order for truth to "set us free" it must first produce within us change, and change will require us to "repent of dead works."

"What are dead works?" you ask. Anything outside His divine destiny for our lives, no matter how good or moral, is a dead work in His sight. I don't care what it is. You may be the greatest Sunday School teacher your church has, but if God hasn't destined you to teach that Sunday School class, then it's a dead work; and on Judgment Day, it's going to burn up!

Please take time to understand this. What you and I do in this life matters a lot. Far more than fulfilling a religious duty, our works are to be a part in His total, eternal plan. God has placed us here with a specific destiny and purpose in His mind. Your responsibility and mine is to discover and fulfill His vision. Anything less is just "dead works" that are going to burn.

Many believers will have a difficult time with what I've just stated because they have not been taught that God is willing to be that involved in their personal lives. Listen, my brother and sister, God is totally consumed with His vision for you and me. He intricately made us, and in so doing, He has placed within each of us unique talents and abilities that will enable us to fulfill His vision for our lives to the fullest. Your job, and mine, is to discover this purpose early on in our walk with the Lord and dedicate our entire earthly life to fulfilling His destiny for us.

By now many may be wanting to scream, "But it's by GRACE not WORKS that God judges us. You know, unmerited favor?" Well, the Bible does emphatically state that it is "by grace through faith" that we have been saved. It also states, however, that "faith without works is dead," and "without faith it is impossible to please God." Further, the scriptures teach, "whatsoever is not of faith is sin." (See James 2:17, and Hebrews 11:6.)

"But, what about GRACE?" Let me give you my definition of grace. For too long we have hidden behind the "unmerited favor" definition and allowed that shallow understanding of grace to keep us from the tremendous responsibility grace affords us. God did not give us grace so that we could do whatever we want to and get Him to bless it. Far from it. Grace, by its very existence, demands much more from us all.

Grace is the empowering presence of God enabling you to do what God has called you to do and to be who God has called you to be. That's grace. Not this "God's Riches At Christ's Expense" stuff. Oh, there's nothing wrong with that definition in and of itself, but grace holds us far more accountable to His lordship than we have been taught to appreciate.

You see, it's by His grace that you and I can achieve our destiny in God and fulfill His eternal plan for our earthly life. I don't know about you, but I want to do something that counts down here. Something that's going to affect the kingdom of God and last throughout all eternity. I am consumed by that one desire. My life is going to be what He desires it to be, and I am going to do completely what He desires for me to do. I am going to fulfill my destiny in Christ.

Do you see what you're doing now as a part of God's eternal plan for your life? I get so frustrated when I hear someone say, "You know, I never really wanted to....". You just fill in the blanks. In my case, I often hear preachers lament that they "never really wanted to be a preacher." Oh, how it must hurt the heart of the Father to hear one of His children say that they are displeased with His divine destiny for their life.

"Well, that's not what I meant," you may be thinking. Then shut up and don't say stupid things like that! My testimony is that there is nothing on earth that I would rather do than preach this glorious gospel and pastor God's flock because I heard Him tell me personally that this is His will for my life. What an honor! What a privilege! I am destined to be one of God's great shepherds! I am carving out a part of eternity that will last because I have embraced and accepted His destiny and vision for my life.

You know what? I'd feel that way if God had called me to be a lawyer, teacher, doctor, construction worker or anyone else. Why? Because the highest calling of God you can attain is to discover His destiny for your life and fulfill it. And, that doesn't mean that you have to be a preacher or missionary. How many times have I sat in a pastor's office to hear him complain about how miserable he is pastoring. "You know, brother," I am often told, "if God weren't making me do this, I'd get out and get a good job." Do you know what my counsel is to them? GET OUT! Get out now before you damage more people than you already have.

God is not looking for some great sacrifice on your part in order to line you up with His destiny. NO! The Bible says that His "yoke is easy and His burden is light." God is not trying to kill you with His will for your life. He is trying to fulfill you and usher you into a place of "joy unspeakable and full of glory." If you hate what you're doing, then one of two things is wrong. Either you are not doing what God desires for you to do, or you have not heard God speak to you directly concerning your assignment and therefore are unable to do it "with your whole heart as unto the Lord." The only way we can do that is to hear Him speak to us personally about what we are to do.

"God will speak to me?" you ask. Well, of course He will. Didn't Jesus Himself state that, "My sheep hear My voice and a stranger's they will not follow"? (John 10:4-5 paraphrased.) God wants to talk to you, and if you are not hearing Him speak, then you are in serious trouble. In fact, I would question your relationship with Christ if you are not hearing Him speak to you.

That got your attention, didn't it? "What do you mean, you question my relationship to the Lord? Who do you think you are?" I can answer that. I am a pastor who desires with all his heart for the members of the Body of Christ to enter into their divine, God-appointed destinies. To do that, however, you must hear from God yourself. Jesus said that this is one way you know that you are truly a believer. He will speak to you, personally. He, Himself, will guide you and direct you into your full destiny by His own voice and Spirit.

Unfortunately, in this day and time, we have become so dependent upon "leadership" telling us what to do, we have forgotten "lordship." Leadership should only confirm what lordship has already spoken, not the other way around. If you want to know God's destiny for your life, ask Him before you ask your pastor, counselor or advisor. He is Lord, and He alone can tell you the whole story.

This is true in every aspect of your life, not just "church stuff." God's destiny demands that He show you His purpose for your marriage, your children, your career and all other aspects of your individual life. The only thing that hinders Him from doing so is our lack of seeking Him and learning to hear His voice.

Think for a moment about familiar Bible characters whose entire lives were totally changed after they tapped into God's destiny for them. Moses was transformed from Pharaoh's scared stepson who ran away and lost himself among some sheep to being the great deliverer of Israel. Joseph became the vessel through which not only his household was saved but the entire land was blessed rather than remaining the spoiled youngest child of an aged Jewish clan leader. David, the shepherd boy, became the greatest king Israel has ever known once he got a glimpse of God's destiny for him. Paul went from being a strict teacher of the law and persecutor of Christians to the apostle of the Gentiles, and through him God left us the majority of the New Testament. On and on the Bible tells of men and women who, once confronted with His destiny for their lives, were transformed from ordinary people to eternal molders of His divine will.

You and I are to become just like them. We are to find and fulfill our destiny. Oh, it may take us our entire lifetime of ten, twenty, forty or a hundred years on this earth to accomplish it, but the joy of knowing that we fulfilled the Father's heart for our lives and that we really made a difference because we submitted to His lordship is more than sufficient to reward our efforts and justify our changes.

Are you submitted to His lordship so that His destiny for you can be fulfilled? Really? Have you placed everything you have, everything you desire and everyone with whom you are involved on the altar to allow Him to judge whether this is in His plan for your life?

What about marriage? Your marriage partner is the single most important person in your life after your relationship with Jesus. Did you marry your spouse because God revealed to you that you were to marry, or did you marry him/her because you "just wanted to."

While most of us will marry at some point in our lives, there are a few that God has called to celibacy. I wonder what would have happened to Paul if he had married a wife? Can't you just imagine her complaining about his frequent trips, many meetings and constant discipling of others, all of which took him away from her? You see, for Paul, God's will was celibacy. There was no way he could have fulfilled God's divine destiny in his life and be married. For him, the plan was to "stay single."

Now, what about you? Why are you married to the person you call "honey"? Is it because you know that he or she is a part of the divine plan, or is it because you just decided you would marry because "it's better to marry than to burn"? Isn't it ironic that the very scripture we use to justify our act of the flesh is ultimately going to come to pass anyway? You see, if your spouse is not a part of your destiny in God, then all the two of you accomplish together, when placed before Almighty God on the day of judgment, is going to burn away just like "wood, hay and straw." Why? Because you did not allow His lordship to rule over that part of your life.

The same holds true for children. Yes, children are indeed "the blessing of the Lord." But, many people have children not because they sought the Lord for His blessing, but simply because that's what married people do. Then they use the kids as a further excuse for not serving the Lord. Had they bothered to consult His lordship regarding their children, they could have spared themselves and their families countless hours of heartache and trouble. You see, His destiny in our lives guarantees us success only if we follow His plan in every area of our lives. Not just "the church stuff" — every area of our lives.

Speaking of "church stuff," why do you attend the church that you currently attend? Destiny in God will join you to the proper body to fulfill you, but most of us never even consider this when looking for a church to join. Usually we base church membership on personal likes and dislikes rather than divine instruction. To perfect us, however, God will use covenant relationships in the church. So, the local assembly we belong to matters a great deal. Wouldn't it be a shame to get to heaven and find that all our "good works were as filthy rags" even though we did them in His name? That's not enough. We must do the works of the One we love not out of religious duty, but rather as a result of understanding our divine destiny. It doesn't matter that we don't like everybody at the church or even that we are recognized as important. What matters is that we are joined where God wants us joined.

No one understands this principle better than I. For years I wanted to leave the church that my father pastored because I didn't believe that I'd ever have a place of ministry there. The only thing that kept me from doing what I wanted to do in my flesh — run away — was God's exceedingly clear word to me, "This is where I've put you." That settled it. If I were never recognized as anything more than a janitor or caretaker, God had destined me to be a part of my father's local assembly. That was His destiny for me.

But now hath God set the members every one of them in the body, as it hath pleased him.
1 Corinthians 12:18

That's it. Not what we want, but what He desires. God knows where the best covenant relationships in our life are going to be formed. Rest in that. Don't fight the will of God, just flow with what He reveals to you by His Spirit.

Are you willing to pay the price to walk in His divine destiny for your life? That's the only way that you and I are going to be totally fulfilled. It's the only way that we are going to "produce fruit which will last." It's the only way that we are going to be greeted by our Lord on that eternal day when He will judge all our works from this life and either say, "Well done, thou good and faithful servant. Enter into the joy of your Lord," or "Depart from Me you worker of iniquity. I never knew you." Which will it be for you?

"It's too late for me, brother," you may be thinking. "I've screwed it all up." Well, I've got some good news for you. It's never too late to change. No matter how many wrong choices you have made, you can change. It begins by getting on your knees and asking God to forgive you for your self-righteous acts and fully submitting to His will and way for your life. God can do wonders with a broken vessel, and He will surely direct you and your life into a dimension that will ultimately allow His destiny to come forth in and through you.

Don't delay! It is totally up to you as to whether you enter into His destiny for your personal life. God holds no one else accountable in making us what we are to ultimately become in Him. On Judgment Day, the excuses that will never work are, "No one told me," or "But, God, they told me to do it this way." The bottom line is this — you and I have a personal, intimate relationship with God, and He holds you and me accountable for the things He has shown and imparted to us. No one else. Just you and me, individually.

If you don't know what His destiny is for you, then begin now seeking Him "while He may be found." God is not trying to "hold out" on you. On the contrary. It is "the Father's good pleasure to give us the kingdom." God's on your side. He wants you to succeed. Start right now. Purpose in your heart that no matter what anyone else does, you are going to discover, pursue and fulfill your divine destiny in God so that His eternal purpose in your life, when judged, will endure the fire and be for you a great reward.

2

Corporate Destiny

Now that we have discovered we have a personal destiny in God, let me challenge you to the next level of discovery. As surely as each individual believer has a claimed destiny from God the Father, so does each local church body. That's right. Every local church has a destiny the Father is waiting for them to fulfill. I call this concept corporate destiny.

Before we can really elaborate on a church's corporate destiny, I must first establish within your thinking a concept that many find quite disturbing. I'm talking about headship. You see, in the Bible the Church is likened to the human body in an attempt for us to better understand God's master plan. And, like the human body, the body of Christ must have a "head" in order for His body to know what to do, where to go, and how to behave. This is known as "headship."

> **But I want you to understand that Christ is the head of every man, and the man is the head of a woman, and God is the head of Christ.**
>
> **1 Corinthians 11:3 NASB**

This verse is one of the most astonishing to me in the entire New Testament. Why? Because it reveals that everyone in this life is designed to have a covering — even Jesus! In fact, as far as I can see from this scripture, God is the only person in the universe Who needs no covering. Everyone else must be covered.

Before I proceed in detail to explain why headship is so very important, let me share some further scripture with you from 1 Corinthians chapter 12 beginning in verse 14. Rather than put it in verse structure, however, allow me to do as the original manuscripts did and put this entire passage into one paragraph of thought.

For the body is not one member, but many.

If the foot should say, "Because I am not a hand, I am not a part of the body," it is not for this reason any the less a part of the body.

And if the ear should say, "Because I am not an eye, I am not a part of the body," it is not for this reason any the less a part of the body.

If the whole body were an eye, where would the hearing be? If the whole were hearing, where would the sense of smell be?

But now God has placed the members, each one of them, in the body, just as He desired.

And if they were all one member, where would the body be?

But now there are many members, but one body.

And the eye cannot say to the hand, "I have no need of you"; or again the head to the feet, "I have no need of you."

On the contrary, it is much truer that the members of the body which seem to be weaker are necessary;

And those members of the body, which we deem less honorable, on these we bestow more abundant honor, and our unseemly members come to have more abundant seemliness,

Whereas our seemly members have no need of it. But God has so composed the body, giving more abundant honor to the member which lacked,

That there should be no division in the body, but that the members should have the same care for one another.

And if one member suffers, all the members suffer with it; if one member is honored, all the members rejoice with it.

> **Now you are Christ's body, and individually members of it.**
>
> **1 Corinthians 12:14-27** NASB

Throughout his epistles to the churches, the Apostle Paul uses illustrations from the natural body to explain how we relate to Christ and His body. Paul uses the parts, joints and functions of the human body to describe how the spiritual body of Christ works and only in understanding this analogy will we be able to embrace God's concept of corporate destiny.

Notice with me, however, that as Paul expounds upon his human body analogy here in 1 Corinthians 12, he suddenly "shifts gears" and seems to begin addressing an entirely different issue. Upon a closer look, however, we discover that he is still talking about the same line of thought.

> **And God has appointed in the church, first apostles, second prophets, third teachers, then miracles, then gifts of healings, helps, administrations, various kinds of tongues.**
>
> **All are not apostles, are they? All are not prophets, are they? All are not teachers, are they? All are not workers of miracles, are they?**
>
> **1 Corinthians 12:28-29** NASB

Now, why would Paul digress in the middle of talking about body members and begin to speak about offices and giftings within that body? You may not like what I'm about to share, but I believe it to be the key to understanding this chapter. As surely as every individual member of our human body is vital to its overall function and performance, without the giftings of the head we would simply be a human "nobody." So, too, the body of Christ. Though we have not heard it taught very often for fear of being misunderstood, the fact of the matter is that every local body has a "head" and until you recognize your leadership as such, you will simply be a "nobody" church.

Already I can hear the objections. "No man tells me what to do. I answer only to God!" Now, wait a minute. Are you sure you're on scriptural ground when you make that statement? As I thoroughly stated in chapter one, every member of the body of Christ is responsible for hearing from God for their own personal, individual destiny. In the Church, however, God has set first apostles, second prophets, and so on. I wonder why He did that?

For you to truly grasp the importance of what I'm attempting to share, you are going to have to "anoint your ears to hear." (See Matthew 11:15.) You see, I have discovered a tremendous truth over the many years that I have traveled preaching this glorious gospel. The degree to which you and I receive something from God is not nearly as dependent upon the anointing of the speaker as it is the anointing upon us to hear. This was even true in the life of Jesus Christ. That's why He was constantly having to say, "Let him who has ears to hear, hear the Word of God." It wasn't the fact that Jesus wasn't anointed; it was the listeners who needed the help. Even the disciples had to be privately instructed concerning the teachings of Jesus and yet Jesus Himself said, "It is given unto you to know the mysteries of the kingdom." Then later, when Jesus and the disciples were alone, they would come and say, "Uh, Lord. About that teaching You gave today. What were You talking about?"

Were the disciples just stupid? No, I don't believe that at all. The disciples were just like you and me. They were so accustomed to their way of doing things, their tradition, that they had a difficult time accepting new concepts that challenged those traditions. That's why Jesus said,

> **You nicely set aside the commandment of God in order to keep your tradition.**
>
> **Mark 7:9 NASB**

That brings us to a major point. In order for us to individually and corporately fulfill our destiny, we must not only be willing to change, we must actually change. "OH, NO! Not that. Anything but that. I can't change. I'm too old. Besides, you ought to know that you can't teach an old dog new tricks!" Well, aren't you glad that you're not an old dog?! Of course you can change. In fact, if you're going to follow Jesus, you have no choice in the matter. Malachi 3:6 declares, **For I am the Lord, I change not.**

Uh-oh. Since scripture states that we are to become "like Jesus" and He does not change, I wonder just who does change? You know the answer to that, don't you? You and I do the changing. Every day that we live with Jesus, we are to become just a little more like Him through the process of change.

I get so concerned when I come upon people who have decided they are not going to change anymore. Their philosophy is usually, "We've always done it this way and that's the way it's going to be!" If ever there were a death sentence hung around a local church or people, that's it. If we believe the Bible when it states, "He is new and fresh every morning," how in God's name are we going to be "new and fresh" with Him if we hang onto yesterday's experiences?

Consider with me for a moment the children of Israel as they were being led by Moses through the wilderness. Can you imagine the trouble they would have been in if they had refused to "change" when God's cloud moved? I can just imagine one of the men digging in, getting secure and becoming familiar with his surroundings after the cloud has led them to a well-watered plain. He's enjoying his new place, and he begins to think about settling down permanently. For several months, all is well, but then one day someone notices that the cloud is moving again and begins to shout: "The cloud is moving! God is making another change. Time to go!"

What would have happened if this man had said, "I don't care. I'm not going! I like it here. I'm comfortable here. I'm familiar with everything here. This is my security. No — I'm not leaving."

I'm sure someone would attempt to reason with him and encourage him to make the change, but he probably would offer further excuses for not changing. Things like, "I'm tired of always moving with this crazy cloud! It's not doing anything but taking us in circles anyway. I'm going to stay right here and let it catch up with me!"

Have you ever known anyone like this? I meet them all the time. Unfortunately, if you and I don't move when God moves, then we cannot experience His provision, blessing, protection and direction — these are "under the cloud."

If there is one thing that Church history should teach us it is that every time there is a new move of God, its "greatest enemy" is the former move of God. I am convinced that in order for the Church to become all she is destined to become we, God's people, must sharpen our listening skills so that we can hear clearly what the Spirit of God is speaking in this, the Church's finest hour. No longer is God going to bless "doing it our way." His way or no way is the only way. So, where do we begin?

The answer, of course, lies within our destiny. As I have already said, every individual believer must come to terms with their personal destiny in God. This can only be achieved as you and I develop an intimate relationship with Christ as our Lord. This must be the top priority in our lives, for there will come a day when we will have to give an account of our accomplishments before Almighty God.

Likewise, just as you and I as individuals will have to stand before God to give account for the stewardship of our destinies, the Book of Revelation offers clear proof that entire churches will stand before the Lamb for an accounting of their corporate destinies.

You see, I believe that Scripture clearly reveals that every local assembly has specific tasks and assignments they are to accomplish together for God. In order to do so, however, every individual member of the assembly must be willing to come under the "headship" of their leaders so as to be a united body moving together in one purpose and one mind. The problems that arise here, however, result from a tremendous ignorance concerning "boundaries" or clear dimensions of authority between these two destinies — the individual's destiny and the destiny of the corporate body where God has placed the individual.

Hosea chapter four and verse six declares, **My people are destroyed for lack of knowledge.** That, in a nutshell, expounds the problem. Most of us in the local church are so ignorant of what the Bible really teaches regarding individual and corporate destiny we not only do not respond to God in these areas, but when challenged we retreat back into our religious traditions and miss the total plan of God. Why? Because to embrace our corporate destiny requires us to submit to the leadership within for local bodies and by necessity see them as God's voice to us in that place.

"Oh, no! I'm not doing that. Man, I've heard all kinds of stories about leaders that abuse members who are in submission to them." I know. So have I, but just because a few have abused the system does not mean that we need to "throw the baby out with the bathwater."

A lot of the fear in this area comes from testimonies of people who lived through the "Shepherding" or "Discipleship Movement" that came into prominence two decades ago. I personally believe it was a genuine move of God; however, it caused some problems because it moved across the boundaries and dimensions of individual destiny. Please understand this: The plan of God makes provision for every local church to discover and fulfill its divine destiny without intruding or infringing on His individual destinies for its members. In fact, God divinely places each member in a local expression of His kingdom just as a subcontractor might hand-pick and assemble a special construction crew to build a unique building. He doesn't do this in order to control your life, but rather to fulfill it to the max.

Obviously, this will require every believer and leader in the church to understand the boundaries of destiny. It's not that hard, really. Individual destiny has to do with what God requires of you personally and corporate destiny deals with the combining of individuals into a local church for the expressed purpose of fulfilling a common destiny together — exactly like your physical body is required to work together though it consists of many members.

When it comes to your vocation in life, where you will live geographically, whom you will marry (or not marry) or whether or not you'll have children, these are areas that you must hear from God for yourself. I don't believe God calls ministers to do what individuals are supposed to do for themselves. As I have already stated emphatically in chapter one, God holds each of us individually responsible to discover and fulfill our personal destiny in Him.

Yes, I believe that God often uses ministers to give "words of encouragement" or "confirmation" but the issue is lordship. Jesus is Lord and He expects you and me to come into such a personal relationship with Him that we will know what our purpose and destiny in life is because He has personally revealed it to us.

No one in leadership should abuse their position in God by assembling a congregation and then telling them the aforementioned things concerning their lives. Can't you just imagine what a mess that would be? "You sir — yes, you in the third row — you are to be an accountant. And you next to him, you will be a nurse. Fifth row back, you'll marry this woman up front here and oh yes, you young man are to be celibate!" EXCUSE ME?! No way, Jose! Don't leave crucial things like that — things that directly affect your individual destiny from God — in the hands of others, no matter how anointed they are or seem to be. You alone must hear God tell you every detail you need to know concerning His personal destiny for your life. Leadership may confirm it, but God must first "speak it."

Now, with that firmly established, let's move on to what corporate destiny is all about and how it works according to God's plan.

If I understand anything about the Scriptures, it seems clear to me that God has always had the desire and goal to have a family. He is "a family God" Who has openly declared His dream to have a nation of priests and a body of spiritual worshippers to share His life and glory now and forever. God longs for a people who are set apart totally for Him.

This being true, why do most of our churches have almost no concept of corporate destiny? The majority of the body of Christ, though vocally acclaiming to being one, live their lives totally unto themselves rather than moving together as a whole body. In fact, many of us think that the Bible was written just for us individually — but it wasn't! Yes, of course there are portions written to us as individuals, but there are also portions written totally to the unbeliever. Further, the majority of the Bible was written specifically to "the family" of God, His Church — not specific individuals within the family, but to the whole body. That being true, then the only way those portions of scripture can come to pass is if the whole body functions as a whole unit and obeys them. It is absolutely impossible for individual believers to fulfill these specific "family covenants."

If you examine God's dealings with Israel in the Old Testament, you will discover that they were unique and different from any other race on the face of the earth. Why? Because God declared a specific, divine destiny for them as a nation before they even existed! And, as those of you who study your Bible know, it was only when Israel moved together as a unit that they were able to fulfill their destiny and secure the provision, blessing and victory God had already promised them.

Individually, David was destined to slay Goliath and allow Israel to defeat the Philistines. When it came time to enter the Promised Land, however, the entire body had to come into one accord. Remember the twelve spies that Moses sent into Canaan to bring him a report of what Israel could expect when they entered to possess it? Joshua and Caleb said, "We are well able to go up and take the country." The other ten, however, said, "No way. We are as grasshoppers in their eyes and we will certainly be destroyed." (See Numbers 13.)

The ironic thing about all this is that God told them in the very beginning that all these "problems" would be in the land but to have no fear for He, Himself, would give them victory. Unfortunately, the people believed the ten rather than Joshua and Caleb and they were not able to possess what was already theirs. Many churches today are just like Israel was. God has given them specific instructions and assignments that He desires for them to complete, but because the people will not get into accord with His will and way, the tasks go uncompleted and the victory, though guaranteed by the Father, remains to be won.

"Fine," you say, "but that was in the Old Testament. The New Testament is different." Oh, really?

The messages to the seven churches in the Book of Revelation, chapters two and three, graphically demonstrate that those local churches each had a unique calling, and they were held accountable for their works as individual churches. The church at Philadelphia had an astounding call and was praised for its faithfulness in completing that calling.

> **And to the angel of the church in Philadelphia write; These things saith he that is holy, he that is true, he that hath the key of David, he that openeth, and no man shutteth; and shutteth, and no man openeth;**
>
> **I know thy works: behold, I have set before thee an open door, and no man can shut it: for thou hast a little strength, and hast kept my word, and hast not denied my name.**
>
> **Behold, I will make them of the synagogue of Satan, which say they are Jews, and are not, but do lie; behold, I will make them to come and worship before thy feet, and to know that I have loved thee.**
>
> **Because thou hast kept the word of my patience, I also will keep thee from the hour of temptation, which shall come upon all the world, to try them that dwell upon the earth.**
>
> **Behold, I come quickly: hold that fast which thou hast, that no man take thy crown.**
>
> **Revelation 3:7-11**

This passage poignantly shows us that churches don't exist by accident — they exist by divine design, and have a corporate destiny as a called-out company of people. Now here's the part you've got to grasp: When God thinks of them and speaks to them, He does it as if He were speaking to and demanding obedience from one person. Whoa! That's quite different than what you and I have been trained to believe. In fact, when most of us hear the pastor or leader of our local church tell us what they have heard from God, our usual response is, "Well, I'll have to pray about that and see what God tells me." Okay, let's consider that, shall we?

If God is going to speak to a local church as one complete body, then how does that body hear Him when there are so many varied members within it? Remember,

God likens His body, the Church, to our physical body. Though we have many different parts with lots of different functions, they all move together directed by the head. The head gives direction and the body makes it happen. Right? Okay.

Our local church "body" is exactly like that. It has to be led by the "head" and that means that we as individual members of the body must come under the authority of the headship gifts that God has given us in our leadership.

During the last ten years, there has been an all-out attack on the concept of authority by the enemy. Yes, there have been some gross abuses of authority in the Church and in secular government, but that doesn't mean the system is wrong. If we decide to ignore God's covering in our lives through our local church leaders we will be found fighting God's order and His blessing will not abide with us in that local assembly.

The "bottom line" here with regard to corporate destiny is simply this: "How much authority do I give someone else over my life?" Most of us have such a fear of covering and headship, that our fear, rather than God's direction, dominates and taints every facet of our lives.

One of my biggest problems as a teenager was in giving God total control of all of my life. Why? Because I was afraid that if I gave God everything then He would make me marry the ugliest woman in the world or else call me to be a missionary in some remote place of the world that I would hate. The reason I thought this way was because I was taught to believe this was God's method of perfecting holiness in us. Really. I was taught that the more we suffered the more like God we would become. Pretty stupid, huh?

Well, it's no more silly than the ignorance running rampant in the Church today regarding headship. I get so tired of people storming into my office for counseling and saying, "Pastor, do I have to do everything my ungodly spouse tells me to do? He says I have to party and get drunk with him. Do I have to submit and obey him?" Frankly, I just want to scream at them and say, "You silly person, NO!"

Christians can be so dumb! There is so much ignorance about the boundaries of authority and headship in the Church today that I often wonder how any of us make it. Questions like, "Do I have to cheat and steal on the job when my boss tells me I have to do it?" and "Do I have to drink poison if the pastor tells me to drink it?" are so ludicrous that one would think everyone would know the answers. But just in case you don't, the answer is NO!

God, unlike some of His people, is not ignorant. He has a wonderful system of checks and balances which ensures us of success in every area of our lives — including our place in His body. It's all pretty simple, really. God is your ultimate Head. Every step of the way, He has given us His Word and His Spirit to teach and guide us to perfect balance in this life. Yes, we do indeed have under-shepherds to whom we are to submit ourselves within the corporate structure but never to the violation of our individual destiny. For instance, I don't know how you feel about it, but if the government ever tells me I cannot pray, then even though one portion of the Bible tells me to submit myself to the authority of government, I will refuse to obey that government when it clearly violates that higher law and authority who is my Head. I do not have to fear authority in the government or the local church. Why? Because since I have come under the lordship of Jesus Christ and have studied His Word, I have come to understand that if anyone asks me to violate my God's moral law then I will say, NO! His authority in my life is higher than the authority of man, and believe it or not, that knowledge in itself sets me free from the fear of authority in this life.

Okay, now that that's settled, let's look at the other side of the issue. When more than one individual is involved, who is responsible to give the direction so that the entire body can function correctly as one?

In our natural families, the Bible is quite clear on authority and headship.

> **Wives, submit yourselves unto your own husbands, as unto the Lord.**
>
> **For the husband is the head of the wife, even as Christ is the head of the church: and he is the saviour of the body.**
>
>

Ephesians 5:22-23
>
> **Children, obey your parents in the Lord: for this is right.**
>
>

Ephesians 6:1

In the family the husband is the head of the wife and together as "one" they are the head of the children. At no time does the Bible teach that men are superior to women or parents to children — all are equal in importance. The difference is in our function. We do not all have the same responsibilities. Though we are equal in value, we are functionally different.

Everyone reading this book understands how this works. In order to have family harmony and unity there are times when all involved must submit to the head of that family even though they may personally dislike the decisions being made based on preference. And, no amount of "spiritualizing" is going to change anything. Headship makes decisions that are necessary for the entire family (body) to remain "on target."

What if you as a parent went to your son's room to ask why he didn't take out the trash, only to hear him say, "Well Dad, I was getting ready to take out the trash, just like you asked me to, when something unbelievable happened! All of a sudden, I saw a hand appear in my room, and it began to write on the wall, Thou shalt not take out the trash ever again, thus saith the Lord!"

I think my response would probably be, "You know son, I sense God saying something to me right now. Oh, yes, I feel God speaking to me with regard to my hands, and I want to lay them on you!"

You see, our ability to "hear" can be impaired due to our "personal preferences." That's why God has established "headship" or "covering" for all of us. It is the direction from our head that assures that the rest of our body will always be doing exactly what it is supposed to be doing and will receive total fulfillment in accomplishment as the job or task gets done.

While most of us understand the concept of headship in family living, this issue of authority and covering seems to get very confusing when it comes to the local church. As a member of a local church, what would be your response to your pastor announcing one Sunday morning from the pulpit, "God spoke to me last night; He wants us to build a building" or "God spoke to me, and He wants us to go into a month of prayer and fasting." I can tell you how most would respond. They would say, "I have to go pray about it to see if God will confirm this thing and make sure that God is really saying this." My question is, pray about what? Pastor's directive has nothing to do with God's moral law in your personal life. It is for the body as a whole. Just who do you think you are to question him?

Are you angry yet? I know some are, but let's examine this issue just a little further before you condemn me to a place for heretics.

Have you ever heard God speak to you? If you have, then answer this question for me: When God spoke to you, what part of your body heard Him speak? I have asked this question dozens of times in meetings and conferences and the majority of the time the answers are, "He spoke to my spirit or heart," or "He spoke to my mind." I have no problem with any of those answers, for those parts of our body are equipped to hear what God says. Let me ask you this, however; have you ever heard God speak to you through your foot? How about your knee? No, then what about your elbow? Well, why not? Why don't we hear the voice of God in these parts of our body? The answer, though simple, is one of the most profound truths you will ever learn in kingdom living. We don't hear through these parts of our body because they are not equipped with the ability to hear. This certainly doesn't make them any less important, they just function differently than our hearing members.

Now, let's relate this illustration to the corporate body of Christ. How does the church, a local body of believers, hear from God so that they can all move together in one accord? Do we just come together and suddenly the audible voice of God booms from heaven, "Thus saith the Lord!"? No, that's not the way God has chosen to lead His Church. Let's look at Ephesians chapter four and see what Paul tells us.

And he gave some, apostles; and some, prophets; and some, evangelists; and some, pastors and teachers;

For the perfecting of the saints, for the work of the ministry, for the edifying (or building up) **of the body of Christ.**

Ephesians 4:11-12

You see, just like our human body is equipped to "hear" so also is the body of Christ equipped to "hear." We recognize these "five-fold offices" as headship gifts that God has placed within the Church for the purpose of bringing it into full unity and maturity, and when it comes to God speaking to the entire body, it is through these "hearing parts" that He will speak.

So, let's return to our illustration. The pastor has announced a direction for the entire church based on what

God has spoken to him, and you have decided to go home and see if that's what God really said. You have decided you must "hear" from God on this matter yourself. Hear what, foot?! Hear what, knee?! Hear what, elbow?! Just what do you expect to hear? Have you forgotten how God speaks to His body? He speaks through the "hearing members" and that's not who you are! Yes, God speaks directly to you concerning your personal destiny, but in the Church He speaks only to headship — never membership. To believe otherwise is to make a complete mockery of the body of Jesus Christ and the One Who carefully crafted it and placed its members and leadership gifts into place. The concept that you and I need to hear God's direction for the whole body of local believers is absurd!

"Well, what if the head makes a mistake? What if they miss it?" Once again, let's look at our physical body for an answer.

Has your head ever made a decision that hurt another part of your anatomy? Mine has. There have been times when my head directed my body to do something that caused a toe to be stubbed or another part of my body to hurt, but you know what? Even though my head made a mistake and caused me some pain, I didn't cut off my head! I didn't resign and say, "I'm leaving my head! I'll never trust it again." I may not be the smartest person around, but I know this. Life with a head is the best thing going! My body may not like or even approve of every decision my head makes, but it understands that without the head there is no life! Without my head, my body would have no direction, no ability to mobilize its many members and absolutely no ability to function at any level that really matters.

Why is the Church world in such a mess today? I believe it is because we have never come to understand the concept of a corporate destiny in God for the local church, and that is because we have never come to fully appreciate and recognize our head.

"But, Jesus is the head of the Church," you reason. I have no problem with that. I agree — Jesus is the head of the Church, but let me ask you a question. Where is Jesus? No, I don't want you to give me a religious answer. I want to know, where is Jesus right now? The answer, of course, is obvious. Jesus is in heaven.

Okay. Now, if Jesus is in heaven, where is His body?

"Well, His body is on earth because scripture states that the Church is His body.

What does that mean, then? Does it mean that the Body of Christ is walking around headless? NO, of course not. Ephesians four makes it clear that God gave headship gifts to men so that His body would be fully covered at all times with the ability to hear and receive direction so that they might fulfill His total plan for their corporate lives.

Our problem is that we just don't recognize these gifts as headship anointings. We usually relegate our pastors to nothing more than servants of our wishes rather than servants of the Most High God. In doing so, we do not see them as the voice of the Lord, but rather as one that we must "keep a close watch on" so that he does what we desire him to do, and nothing more.

The greatest travesty that I have witnessed in this nation's churches is the people of God reducing the mouthpiece that God has placed in their midst to someone who simply shares a word and gives the Bible study. If people like what they hear from this muffled head, they have a tradition of walking out of the assembly and telling their head, "That was really a good word. I enjoyed it." If they didn't like what they heard, they just simply walk by and chat about the weather or some other trivial event.

WHAT A JOKE! God's mouthpiece reduced to nothing but a "preacher on a leash."

Compare that to the children of Israel under Moses. When they heard the voice of God, who did God sound like? According to the Bible, God sounded like Moses and because God sounded like the "voice" they were familiar with, it made it that much easier to recognize it as God's voice to them.

Our problem is that we don't recognize the man or woman that God has given to lead us as His mouthpiece. We don't know who our leaders really are.

Some time ago, the Rev. E.V. Hill preached a message in our church entitled, "A Church That Matters." That sounds like a really good title, doesn't it? I have to be honest and tell you that we were not quite ready for what this man of God had in mind. He stood up and declared, "You know, the great majority of all the churches in America don't matter!" I can assure you he had our attention. He said this because he knows that most churches look at the person behind the pulpit without really knowing or recognizing who that man or woman is in God. They don't understand that only through God's chosen mouthpiece can they realize and receive a revelation of their corporate destiny.

I want to reemphasize a point I shared earlier in this chapter. The degree to which you and I receive something from God is not nearly as dependent on the anointing of the speaker as it is on our anointing, or ability, to hear what's being said. Let me illustrate.

Would you agree with me that Jesus Christ was the most anointed minister Who ever has or ever will live? I certainly believe this to be true. Everywhere Jesus went He performed amazing miracles, healed the sick by the thousands, fed the multitudes with only a handful of food and spoke with such love and authority that the wisest to the simplest were at ease in His presence. This man could not only "draw a crowd," He could keep them! Except in one place, Nazareth.

> **But Jesus said unto them, A prophet is not without honour, but in his own country, and among his own kin, and in his own house.**
>
> **And he could there do no mighty work, save that he laid his hands upon a few sick folk, and healed them.**
>
> **And he marvelled because of their unbelief. And he went round about the villages, teaching.**
>
> **Mark 6:4-6**

What a tremendous, yet horrific, revelation. Jesus Christ, the Son of Almighty God, anointed by God to do "good works," was totally hindered from doing all the Father desired for Him to do in Nazareth. Why? Because of the people's unbelief — they refused to recognize Jesus for who He was. Rather than accept the fact that He was the Son of God, they reasoned, "Why, this is Mary and Joseph's boy. You know, He always has been a little strange. Besides, can any good thing come out of Nazareth?" How stupid! Jesus, Himself, hindered because the people refused to recognize who He was to them.

Now, consider this: If God Himself couldn't do any mighty works in the midst of people who refused to recognize Him, then how can a man or woman of God do anything when the members of the church won't recognize who they are or who sent them?

At one point early in my ministry, God sent me on an assignment to find out why the largest churches in the nation have succeeded. I visited many of the "megachurches" of today pastored by the likes of Jerry Falwell, Robert Schuller, Earl Paulk, Tommy Reid, John Gimenez and Jack Hayford. As I studied their concepts of church government, worship and outreach ministry I saw quickly that these were not the reason for their greatness. In fact, as I searched for the "common denominator" that all great churches have, I soon discovered that neither doctrine nor denominational affiliation had anything to do with their success. As far as I could see, there was only one thing that all these churches, diverse as they were, had in common — the people in these churches understand and believe that their pastor is the mouthpiece of God for their corporate destiny.

They may not say it the way I've described it, but if you visit these churches, you'll see the evidence. If you visit Jerry Falwell's church, don't think that you can stand in the lobby and say slanderous things about Pastor Falwell — you won't get out the same as you came in! Jack Hayford's people will not allow you to speak against their mouthpiece. They protect the servant of God, for they understand he is the one through whom God will give them all direction as a body.

Is this idol worship? No, these people worship God, not the mouthpiece God has given to them. They just understand God's order for their church to be blessed.

Okay. That brings us to looking much more closely at these headship gifts that God has given His Church. Just who is the "head honcho" in the church? To really understand this, we must once again put aside our "traditions" and look to the Word for instruction.

Our tradition tells us that the pastor is the only one who can be the "head honcho" in the local church. Only the pastor, or pastor/teacher, is recognized by most believers as the supreme authority in a local assembly. The problem with that is you can't validate it anywhere in the Word of God, yet it is a major part of the American church tradition. The fact of the matter is, God often places the other leadership gifts in the office of chief elder.

To restate Paul's writing,

> **And God hath set some in the church, first apostles, secondarily prophets, thirdly teachers, after that miracles, then gifts of healings, helps, governments, diversities of tongues.**
>
> **1 Corinthians 12:28**

I wonder why Paul didn't write this passage to line up with our "tradition?" Surely, he must understand that the pastor is the "official" head of the local church. I'm sorry if you don't like what I'm teaching you, but the truth is that nowhere in Scripture is the pastor said to be the head. In fact, any church that does not touch an apostolic or prophetic ministry is a church that will never be able to build or successfully achieve anything of lasting value. Why? Because it is totally void of any foundation. Check it out in your own Bible, every church that was birthed in the New Testament was birthed through an apostolic or prophetic ministry. There was absolutely no concept of birthing a church without these ministries.

Does this mean that the person who is the head of an assembly has to be an apostle or a prophet? No, however, it does mean that somehow every local church has to be aligned with those gifts if they want to have a solid foundation upon which to build.

I can hear the screaming now. "You listen to me, brother, Jesus is the only foundation that our church is built upon!" I understand your concern. I totally agree that Jesus is indeed the Rock of our existence, and in Him and by Him everything exists, but I urge you to read your Bible more closely. According to the Word of God, Jesus has ordained the apostle and prophet as the foundation of His Church on earth — Jesus is the Chief Cornerstone Who ties it all together!

> **Now therefore ye are no more strangers and foreigners, but fellowcitizens with the saints, and of the household of God;**

> **And are built upon the foundation of the apostles and prophets, Jesus Christ himself being the chief corner stone;**
>
> **In whom all the building, fitly framed together groweth unto an holy temple in the Lord.**
>
> **Ephesians 2:19-21**

You see, the way you view someone affects what you will receive from them. If you see your leadership in the local church as nothing more than "hired servants," then you will respond to them as hired help. But, if you see your leaders as God's voice to your body, then you will begin to support and cherish them so that all God had destined for you as a body can come to pass.

Let's look at Jesus again for clarity in this issue. In the gospel of Mark, Jesus looked at His disciples and asked,

> **Whom do men say that I am?**
>
> **And they answered, John the Baptist: but some say, Elias; and others, One of the prophets.**
>
> **Mark 8:27-28**

Then Jesus asked the most important question — the one that revealed the truth the whole Church is built upon: **But whom say ye that I am?** It was then that Peter answered with a revelation straight from the throne of heaven, **Thou art the Christ** (Mark 8:29).

It is absolutely imperative for us, the Church, to begin to see our leadership for who they truly are. Anything less than seeing and receiving them in their anointed "mouthpiece" positions will hinder us from becoming all God has destined us as a body to become. Not only that, but the servants of God themselves will become so discouraged in attempting to "prove" themselves, they may just decide to quit!

I have met countless prophets and apostles who started churches, but finally ended up giving them away to others, even though the churches had grown to include thousands of people. Why? They were grieved because they were never received or allowed to function as God's gifts so they could satisfy the calling of God in their churches. They literally had to travel somewhere else to find people who would receive them. They were frustrated, depressed and deeply disappointed because their people never released them in their calling, and unfortunately, every year that passes sees more leadership gifts leaving the churches they founded because of this problem.

On the other hand, when a corporate body does begin to understand who it is that stands in their midst as God's voice to them, they will immediately begin to notice significant change. First, their prayer lives will change. With this new knowledge and direction, the church will find much of its prayer life redirected by the Holy Spirit toward the man or woman who is God's gift to their assembly. Instead of occupying an hour with endless "wish" alias "prayer" lists, the people will pray earnest prayers with a common theme.

"Dear Lord God, I want to know what Your will for my life is in this church family. Lord, I pray for that leader; reveal through Your servant, Father, what our destiny is as a people. Reveal to us what our destiny is in this community, this state, this nation and the world. Father, we are hungry to know what we were created to do as a church family. We purpose to hear and obey Your call. In Jesus' name."

Now, if we are going to begin to accept our leadership for who they are, we must decide which of the headship offices we are willing to acknowledge as active in the church today.

"Well sir, we accept the pastor." Yeah, I know. Everybody and his brother think they know what the "pastor" is supposed to do. Honestly, that's the one title I prefer not to go by because, when people think they understand a thing, then they think they can judge, direct and "improve" that thing. You know as well as I do that everybody has advice for the pastor as to how he or she can be a better shepherd, and of course, everyone is comfortable using the label "pastor" when addressing him or her. "God bless you, Pastor," is something that is heard in churches across the land every time we meet. We will address him by his title with no hesitation whatsoever. Many of us will even recognize the teacher and openly say, "My goodness, child, you are a teacher sent from God for this house. God bless you." Furthermore, until recently we openly acknowledged the office of the evangelist though now, due to all the "bad press" the evangelist has received, many churches are choosing just to call them a "guest speaker" or "traveling pastor."

But, what about the apostle and prophet? When was the last time you heard someone say, "God bless you, prophet," or "God bless you, apostle"? If you have ever heard it, I would be surprised. "Oh, but you don't understand, Brother Meares, we're not into titles. I mean, we don't have to use titles because titles aren't important. You know, we're all just brothers and sisters in Christ here."

Is that so? Well, I disagree completely. I think titles are important — in fact — I think titles are very important.

Recently in a meeting, I walked over to a cute little girl on the front row and asked, "Do you belong to someone here, sweetheart?" Instantly, that precious child spoke up and said, "Yes, I'm with my mommy and daddy," and she pointed to her parents seated next to her. I asked the girl's father and mother what their names were, and then I tried my best to "correct" this misled young lady who apparently didn't know her parent's names but only their titles.

"Who is this?" I asked her.

"That's my mommy," she replied.

"Oh, no dear. That's not Mommy. That's Jane. Her real name is Jane and this man, he's Tom. See — this is Jane, and this is Tom. Now, who is this?"

"That's my mommy!"

"And, who is this man?"

"That's my daddy!"

"Now wait a minute, dear — this man just told me his name is Tom. Why don't you call him Tom?"

After a cute little giggle that made me feel like the fool I was portraying, the little girl answered with the wisdom that only God can give: "I call him Daddy because he is my daddy!"

I don't know how you feel as a parent, but I don't let my kids call me Don either. Why? Because in addressing me by my title as Dad, my children are expressing far more than that title. They are expressing my function in their lives and their relationship to me which we both cherish together. Titles help express a degree of receptivity of how a person and office are functioning in our lives. Many may call me Don, but only my kids get to call me Dad!

Only the most foolish of believers would dare to say that titles are not important. Why do you think the early "apostles" moved in such miraculous power and authority? It was because the people understood who these men were in their lives and therefore were prepared and fully expectant to receive from them. This was so true in the Apostle Peter's life that just the very passing of his shadow produced miracles for the people! I can't imagine the people being so casual with him as to say, "Hey, Pete! How's it going?" Oh, no, far from it. In fact the Bible states that the anointing among the apostles was so great and so recognized that "great fear" was upon the people and many miracles were done "by the hands of the apostles." Isn't it about time for this level of anointing to return to our local fellowships? The only way that it can is for the membership of that assembly to recognize the headship gifts that are among them and receive them accordingly.

Let me share with you why I believe this so strongly. My natural father, who is also my father in the Lord, is a silver-haired, elderly gentleman who is one of the most gracious, kind and generous men I know — totally different from me! He also happens to be one of the finest pastors you will ever meet. He'll pray for you when you're sick, visit you in the hospital, and he'll even take your phone calls at his house at three or four o'clock in the morning! (You wouldn't dare want to try that with me!)

I grew up watching people tell him their problems by the hour, year after year. He was a "pastor's pastor" for the first 24 years of his ministry in our church in Washington, DC. But even though he gave it "all he had," the ministry didn't seem to accomplish much in all those years. We conducted every evangelistic program that you could possibly have; we went door to door, we had the proverbial bus ministry, we did everything. It didn't matter. It seemed no one even knew we were in the city, just as no one knows about most of the churches in the city where you live! I can still remember the day all that changed.

A company of prophets came and stood up and pointed their "bony fingers" at the people and rebuked us: "Here in your midst is an apostle of God. He is revered and respected and received all over this nation and around the world, but in this assembly you see him as nothing but a pastor."

You cannot begin to imagine the wonderful change that occurred in our church after the prophets rebuked us for not knowing who this man was in our lives. Once we believed enough to see and receive my father's supernatural calling, once we submitted to God and elevated our mouthpiece to what God had called him to be, overnight it seemed our ministry exploded!

Now people know us wherever we go. Whenever we have a special function, we don't have to invite the city dignitaries but we will often see the mayor, city council and other civic leaders seated comfortably among our people. We have quit trying to "win friends and influence people." We are busy fulfilling our destiny in God, because we have put our house in His proper order. We are letting Jesus build our church His way for we know that if God doesn't build the house, all our labor is in vain.

How is the foundation of the "house" you are joined to? Is the relationship of the apostle and prophet secure within its foundation? Without an apostolic and prophetic vision, the best a local assembly can do is "maintain until death." No, not because these offices are more important than the pastor and teacher. All of the five-fold offices are equal in value, they are just functionally different and the offices of apostle and prophet are imperative for the foundation to be strong enough for the pastor, teacher and evangelist to build upon.

If you want to see your church experience revival, if you desire for your local assembly to complete her God-given destiny as a body, if you want power that will produce miracles for your "house" regularly, then pray fervently for God's anointing on the mouthpiece He has placed in your local church and treat him accordingly. Only then will you begin to see your corporate destiny come to pass.

3

God's Pattern of Joining

No discussion of destiny and purpose would be complete without thoroughly examining a major principle and pattern established for us in both the Old and New Testaments which I refer to as "God's pattern for joining." While most of us have never been taught these concepts, the Bible is filled with illustration after illustration of how these "joining" principles work for our benefit—both individually and corporately. I believe how we respond to our knowledge of "joining" will directly affect our destiny in God.

Let's look at a discussion Jesus had with a group of religious leaders:

> **For this cause shall a man leave father and mother, and shall cleave to his wife: and they twain shall be one flesh. Wherefore they are no more twain, but one flesh. What therefore God hath joined together, let not man put asunder.**
>
> **Matthew 19:5-6**

This verse reveals the "joining" principle as well as any verse in the Bible, and it serves as one of the foundational principles upon which the entire Church is meant to be built: When God joins something (someone) together, don't try to separate it (them). The Father has specific reasons for joining us individually and corporately to those that He has established in our lives, and we would be wise to strengthen these relationships rather than wrestle with them.

In Ephesians, the Apostle Paul reiterates the joining principle by once again using marriage as the illustration.

However, he takes it one step further than just one on one relating to our spouses:

For this cause shall a man leave his father and mother, and shall be joined unto his wife, and they two shall be one flesh. This is a great mystery: but I speak concerning Christ and the church.

Ephesians 5:31-32

The lesson to be learned here is obvious. Our marriages in the natural are to teach us and give us greater insight into our relationship with Christ and His Church. All of us who have been married for any length of time realize that marriage brings out certain things within us that we didn't know were there — both good and bad. The closer to Jesus we walk in fulfillment of our God-designed destiny, the more our lives will produce some things we weren't expecting.

One of the things it will produce is an understanding of some of our Lord's most important lessons that He personally tried to convey while on earth. You see, Jesus didn't just come to planet earth to "show off" and amaze us with some miracles — oh, no! Jesus came with a very specific mission in mind and as you read through the gospels, if you will be very observant, you will discover Him time and again stating exactly what His mission was in very clear precise statements. I call these "mission statements." For example, Jesus declared,

I am come that they might have life, and that they might have it more abundantly.

John 10:10

That is a mission statement. Another such statement is in Luke 19:10 where Jesus says, **For the Son of man is come to seek and to save that which was lost.** Elsewhere, John wrote, "For this purpose the Son of God was manifested, that he might destroy the works of the devil" (1 John 3:8b). Mission statements! Any time that you discover one of these take the time to give yourself to them and adopt them as your own definition of how Christ will work with you in His "mission" within your life and destiny.

In my opinion, one of the most astounding mission statements in the Bible appears in Matthew 20:28, for it has life-changing implications for every servant of God in the local church!

Even as the Son of man came not to be ministered unto, but to minister, and to give his life a ransom for many.

What an incredible revelation. Jesus did not come to be ministered to, but to minister to someone. So, the question becomes: who did He come to minister to?

The Greek word translated here as "minister" is diakoneo, from which we get our word for "deacon." It literally means "to wait on another; to serve." Jesus did not come to be waited on, He came to wait on somebody — to serve them. Who did He come to serve?

If I were to ask this question of the people where you go to church, the majority of them would say, "Well, it's pretty obvious, isn't it? Jesus came to wait on and serve the people. Everybody knows that!" Would you be shocked if I were to tell you that is absolutely incorrect? Jesus' first priority was not to serve the people! Although Jesus did indeed minister to the needs of people throughout His ministry, He was never controlled or driven by the needs of the people.

Most Christians have the concept that Jesus was constantly in the "ministry mode," and that anytime He saw or heard of a need, He just had to respond and meet that need. If Jesus saw a sick person, many of us feel that He just couldn't help Himself but had to run right over to that sick person and say, "HEAL!" I mean, after all, He was Jesus and He always healed everybody, right? Nope!

Jesus Christ is the only man I've heard of Who could be ministering in a "healing line" where everybody was really being healed and halfway through the line, He would get into a boat and sail to some other place! Can you imagine what would happen to a minister who tried that today, if in fact everyone was being healed, and he or she just left the meeting without another thought? Why, the people would literally riot. They'd begin to scream and shout, "Come back here, you! I haven't gotten my healing yet. Where do you think you're going?"

Jesus is the only minister I know Who could go to the equivalent of a modern-day hospital and only heal one person, like He did at the pool of Bethesda in John 5:2-13, and walk away from all the other sick people there with absolutely no sense of guilt and no condemnation about those other people's needs. How can this be?

Our problem lies within our shallow and very incomplete picture of Jesus and His mission. While most see Him as the One Who meets every need the moment that need arises and is always sweet and kind, the Bible reveals quite another side to His nature. For instance, Jesus is the only man I know Who could look a woman straight in the eye and say, "You are a dog" (as He did the Canaanite woman in Matthew 15:22-28). I wonder what would happen if your pastor said that to a lady in your church? You know what would happen. He'd be given "the left foot" of fellowship!

Accordingly, Jesus did not have a lot of disciples. In fact, Jesus didn't have a very large "congregation" at all. Oh, sure, He had large crowds follow Him, but the Bible makes it very clear that they followed Him for the loaves and the fishes — the miracles. Even when someone did volunteer to "hang with Him," He often didn't respond the way we believe He should.

Remember the story in Luke 9:59-60 where one man said, "Jesus, I will pay the price to be Your disciple. I want to follow You." So Jesus said, "Fine, follow Me." Then the man said, "My dad just died, Lord, let me go bury him first." Jesus' response shatters the image we have created for Him by saying, "Let the dead bury their dead." Wow! There's no doubt in my mind that you can mark that disciple off the list. He's gone!

Another time Jesus seemed to "step over the line" was when He was addressing the seventy disciples who had been sent out to work miracles. He told them,

> **Verily, verily, I say unto you, Except ye eat the flesh of the Son of man, and drink his blood, ye have no life in you.**
>
> **John 6:53**

The disciples didn't understand what He was talking about. They thought He was talking about cannibalism, and they reacted exactly like many of the leaders in local churches do today when they hear their pastor say something they don't like: "Okay, that's it. That's enough! We are not going to do this. We're out of here." And, that's exactly what these seventy did. They left Him.

After most of them had gone, Jesus turned to the twelve and said, **Will ye also go away?** (John 6:67) and Peter very wisely said,

> **Lord, to whom shall we go? thou hast the words of eternal life.**
>
> **And we believe and are sure that thou art that Christ, the Son of the living God.**
>
> **John 6:68-69**

The twelve might not have understood all that Jesus taught, but they knew better than to "jump ship" midstream. Besides, Peter stated, where would they go? They'd given all they had to Jesus. Their commitment was one hundred percent.

Speaking of money, Jesus is the only preacher with the guts to actually give an altar call where He said to the rich young ruler, "If you want to be perfect, fine. Give all of your money to the poor." (See Matthew 19:18-24.) Money was obviously something the young man couldn't surrender to the lordship of Jesus because the Bible says he did not obey Jesus' instruction.

The only reason Jesus could do these "unorthodox" things is that He was never controlled by the needs of the people. Contrary to our traditional thinking, Jesus did not "jump" every time someone said, "Meet my need now!" In fact, when it came to religious people of His day, Jesus was especially hard on them. He publicly called them snakes, vipers, "the blind leading the blind," and white tombs filled with putrid flesh and bones. I'm sorry, but the Jesus I see in the Word is not skipping through the streets of Jerusalem all the time with carefully blow-dried hair as depicted in the movies. Jesus had a tough message, and He was committed to delivering it whether it was received or not. How could He do this and not experience frustration and depression from all the rejection and misunderstanding? Simple — He was never controlled by the needs of the people.

I will never forget the day the Lord showed up in my office several years ago. I was so-o-o busy for Him. I was counseling people from 9:00 in the morning to 10:00 at night. I was meeting needs. I was becoming the hero of our congregation — or so I thought. When the Lord spoke to me, however, I realized just how "out of control" I was. "What about Me?" He said. "You no longer have any time for Me."

It was at this moment that I realized one of the greatest spiritual truths the Lord has ever taught me: "To be controlled by the needs of the people is to be out of control!"

Any pastor reading this book, please hear this. There is no way you can ever have the fear of the Lord (which is the beginning of wisdom) and have the fear of man. If you are "need-controlled" by the people, you will never be "Spirit-controlled" in responding to them according to His plan and purpose, and the reason so many of you pastors and leaders are need-controlled is because the people believe that your primary purpose is to meet their needs.

One of the best biblical illustrations of a leader being destroyed by becoming need-controlled is Saul, the first king of Israel. Saul was a great king who stood head and shoulders above all the people in his kingdom. The people loved him, but God rejected him. Why? What did Saul do that caused God to declare, "Saul, I reject you because you have rejected Me"? (See 1 Samuel 15:23.) Saul certainly had not committed any great sin such as we see ministers being rejected for today by the Church and its present standards. He had not committed adultery or murdered anyone. He hadn't stolen all the money in the kingdom and, in fact, done any of the things that we think are good reasons to kick pastors and church leaders out of their pulpits and leadership positions.

Saul's subjects loved him as their king, because he satisfied their wants. That's the reason they had desired a king in the first place. They thought a king would be more sensitive to their needs than the invisible God and His bony-fingered prophets. No more would they have to be accountable to God for their destiny. No, sir! They were going to "be like everybody else." (See 1 Samuel 8:19.)

So, what great sin motivated God to tell Saul's personal minister, the Prophet Samuel,

> **It repenteth me that I have set up Saul to be king: for he is turned back from following me, and hath not performed my commandments. And it grieved Samuel; and he cried unto the Lord all night.**
> **1 Samuel 15:11**

Saul forgot that he was the king of God's people, not Saul's people. God put him in leadership to lead, not to please. Parents who please their children by providing all their wants may avoid crying and discomfort for a short season, but they will reap the whirlwind and a lifetime of tears and distress when their spoiled children grow up to be unrestrained, undisciplined, lawless hellions whose whole world revolves around themselves and their needs and wants.

The same truth applies to leadership in the Church — Church leaders are set in place by God to lead, not to please. They are anointed to equip God's people for spiritual work, not to coddle and ensure eternal childhood and selfishness among the redeemed.

The Lord rejected Saul because he loved to please the people more than his God. We confidently tell people that God is a God of everlasting mercy and lovingkindness, and I believe He is, but He is much more than just a one-sided Being. He is also perfectly just and wise. He doesn't care how much we cry and whine, He is determined to bring us to adulthood, whether we like it or not.

Chapters 15 and 16 of the Book of 1 Samuel make it very clear that Saul's biggest concern — now watch this, pastor, elder or deacon — was to do what he felt the people wanted. "The people want me to sacrifice and worship, Samuel, so why don't you just go with me one more time to sacrifice and worship? Come on, I know I made a little mistake, but let's do what the people want so they won't be upset or anything." (See 1 Samuel 15:21-25.) Saul's pitiful attempt at repentance was seen by God as the deception it was, and He went straight to the heart of the matter in confronting Saul.

In the end, God's decree was sobering for anyone in a leadership position in His kingdom. The moment you are controlled by the needs of the people more than the desires of your God, your leadership days are over! By the same token, if your heart is fixed on His will and ways, then even your greatest mistakes are covered by His anointing in your life.

Let's look at God's hand-picked replacement for Saul — David. I am convinced that if David were around today, nobody would let him in their pulpit. This guy was an adulterer and a confessed murderer. He didn't just kill Uriah, he was also personally responsible for the death of a whole bunch of people! This dude was a biblical "Rambo," a killing machine. Yet, there was something about David that motivated our God to say one of the most unusual statements in the Bible:

> **And when he had removed him [King Saul], he raised up unto them David to be their king; to whom also he gave testimony, and said, I have found David the son of Jesse, a man after mine own heart, which shall fulfill all my will.**
>
> **Acts 13:22**

God called David "a man after Mine own heart" not because he had never sinned, but because he had committed terrible sins and was quick to repent. The reason God delighted in David was due to his heart being fixed on God and His ways rather than being fixed on becoming the most popular king with the people as a result of doing everything they wanted him to do. To really become the leader God desires us to be, we must never allow ourselves to "bow to the needs of the people" as opposed to "bowing our knees to God."

Though the Bible teaches explicitly that David, like Jesus Christ, was not controlled by the people and their needs, most Christians and Church leaders do not realize or believe that. The majority of people in the Church today believe that needs and needs being met are their number one responsibility in serving the Lord. This, I believe, is the primary reason most churches "never matter" as E.V. Hill teaches. You cannot become what God wants you to be if you are constantly worried about people and their personal preferences.

Every day in local churches across this nation, people are ordained into the office of deacon who are wonderful church members and who seem to meet all the qualifications of Scripture — they are faithful, they are loyal, and they are available. Then these deacons are put in charge of various departments because of their faithfulness, their abilities, or because of the character seen in them.

Likewise, people are sought out and ordained who seem to meet the biblical qualifications of an elder and great joy is had by the pastor as he/she watches them grow. This same pastor will spend years imparting his or her life to them as they are trained and discipled in the vision for their local church. The irony of this is that almost all church splits come from elders, deacons and other church leaders. In fact, nearly all of the divisions that spring up in our local churches come from leadership. Why is this happening? What is it that we are missing? I believe the root of the problem lies within our misunderstanding of God's principles of joining and serving.

The first deacons in Church history were selected after the church in Jerusalem discovered that certain widows in the congregation were not being fed properly. Far more than a food problem, this was a racial problem because the Grecian widows were being neglected in favor of Jewish widows, and all of us know how nasty those type of situations can become. When the apostles and elders finally heard about it, they decided to search for seven men **of honest report, full of the Holy Ghost and wisdom** to appoint **over this business** (Acts 6:1-3). I think the combination of qualities is significant because you can have a lot of people who are full of the Holy Ghost and "dumb as a box of rocks!"

Once these seven men had been chosen, then the apostles and elders created and ordained this office of the diaconte or deacon. Their purpose was to minister and serve somebody, but just who were they to serve?

If I were to ask the deacons in the average church, "As a deacon, what is your first priority of ministry?" most of them would probably answer, "My first priority is to meet the needs of the people, to serve the people." NO, NO, NO! That is the fallacy that is hurting the Church more than any other. Deacons were never meant to "meet the needs and serve the people" as their first priority. I can hear many of you now, "Well, of course they were! Read it for yourself. The widows were being neglected and the apostles needed someone to meet the needs of those poor, precious women." WRONG!

I realize that I've just dropped a major bombshell on the most popular and accepted idea of Church government in existence, but God's way just doesn't fit into our comfortable tradition. Why did the founding apostles create the office of deacon? Let's go back to the scripture and look more closely at what the apostles really wanted.

The problem in Acts 6 was quite serious. The neglected widows needed to be fed, but the infant Church also had an eternal destiny to fulfill. The apostles faced a simple but serious choice between serving tables or giving themselves completely to God's Word.

> **Then the twelve called the multitude of the disciples unto them, and said,**
>
> **It is not reason that we should leave the word of God, and serve tables.**
>
> **Acts 6:2**

These men made their decision based on one of the most important principles a man or woman of God can ever learn: Anything that will move us out of our purpose will cause us to miss what God called us to do. They refused to allow an urgent need to distract them or take them out of their God-ordained purpose.

I wonder how many pastors have been totally diverted from their calling because they have yielded to the expectations of others by being the janitor of their churches, by doing all the hospital visitation, by doing all of the counseling, by doing all of the work around the church except for the leadership duties of studying the Scriptures and praying.

The apostles didn't ignore their problem, and they didn't make it worse by jumping in to serve the tables themselves. They found "seven men full of the Holy Ghost and of wisdom," and the seven's major responsibility was to wait on or serve the apostles — not just the widows at the tables. These deacons' primary responsibility was to deal with any congregational problem that popped up and would take the leaders away from their calling. These deacons were "joined" to the apostles to "serve" them.

The greatest service and ministry these first deacons could give the local church at Jerusalem was to ensure that its leaders could continue to hear from God. Now get this: Even though the deacons did wait on tables and serve the people; even though the did love and nurture the flock of God, they had been supernaturally joined to the apostles. Their authority to minister and their marching orders came from leaders who were consumed with fulfilling God's vision. These deacons loved the people in the church, and they were involved with meeting their needs most of the time. However, the bottom line was that they were servants under assignment to the voice of God through the leadership, not controlled or motivated by the needs or affections of the flock.

The reason we have so many problems within our churches is because most deacons and leaders believe that they are joined to the people. They think their highest calling is to meet the needs of the people. So they listen to what the people say, they learn what the people want, they weigh their opinions about why the pastor is wrong. Before long, those deacons or leaders show up in the pastor's office with their accusing fingers pointed at the senior pastor defending the needs of the people against "the insensitive and uncaring pastor who spends all of his time praying." These men and women don't have the foggiest idea of what God's destiny is for the church — they're out on a mission of their own design. They're "protecting" the sheep from the shepherd. How stupid!

If you don't get anything else out of this chapter, get this: When deacons and leadership become joined to the needs of the people more than to the purposes of God, they often create strife and division because they also expect the pastor to choose the needs and wants of the people over God's destiny for the church.

The church in America does not understand Church growth the way the Bible teaches it. Scripture declares that God builds His house through multiplication. Our nation is filled with churches created or enlarged by man in God's name, and the method used is division.

The Bible says,

> **Now I beseech you, brethren, mark them which cause divisions and offences, contrary to the doctrine which ye have learned; and avoid them.**
>
> **Romans 16:17**

Unfortunately, most church members would rather "follow" the divisive brother than "mark" him, and that is why so many of our churches never fulfill their destiny in God. Jesus said,

> **Every kingdom divided against itself is brought to desolation; and every city or house divided against itself shall not stand.**
>
> **Matthew 12:25**

It doesn't matter if 50 percent of the house is divided or only 2 percent — a house divided cannot stand. Only through unity will the power of God be released to touch your community and your city for Jesus. Only through unity will your church grow to become the great "voice" that God has destined it to be in your community and geographical area. And of this I am certain, unity will never prevail in a church where the deacons and leadership have never been taught that their biblical priority is to be joined to their mouthpiece, the ruling elder, and to take care of anything that removes or distracts their leader from God's ordained purpose.

After many years of both observation, as an associate in ministry, and implementation, as the senior pastor, I have come to a personal conviction that is absolute in my life and ministry. I will never have an elder, a deacon, a church leader, department head or staff employee in our church who is not a personal gift to me from the hand of God. Why do I feel so strongly? Because if I do accept someone whom God has not given to me, it amounts to my being unequally yoked and my entire purpose in God will be hindered and possibly destroyed due to my being improperly joined.

Remember, the Bible likens people being joined to each other in ministry as "marriage partners." All of us understand how very important it is for us to marry the right mate. Our spouse is the most important person in our lives with the exception of our relationship to Jesus Christ. From our spouse we draw strength, receive support, endure hardships, overcome pressures, maintain balance and perspective, and grow together to become the "one" God intends for us to be. Ministry "joinings" are just as important. Entire local church destinies as well as individual destinies have been aborted due to "unequal" joinings.

This is particularly true when it comes to elders relating properly to their senior pastors, because just like in marriage, these elders' duties require them to get much closer to the pastor than most people in the church; and like marriage, closeness reveals weakness both in mind and body. Suddenly, the elder who had the unrealistic beliefs concerning "the superior holiness and righteous life" of their pastor is confronted with the reality that pastors are as human as the next person! Now, what does one do?

In solving any relationship problem, it is always helpful to remind ourselves of the definition of the role we have in the relationship. So, what is an elder's first priority? The chief responsibility of the elders is to understand that they are personal gifts of God to His mouthpiece in the local church. This enables them to catch the vision from the ruling elder and mouthpiece, not fight over what vision should be followed. Elders catch the vision from their leader, and their job is to amplify the vision and then to implement the vision in the local church.

The problem comes when these elders allow themselves to be joined to the people more than to their "mouthpiece" and the vision God has given that leader for their "house." They often begin to put more weight and value on what the people have to say than on what the Lord is saying through His mouthpiece, the pastor, about the destiny of the local church. This enables the enemy, the devil, to come right in to the midst of God's people and totally destroy their corporate destiny in Him. Only in unity can a house stand and accomplish all it is intended to do. That's why God only gives the vision of the house to one man, the mouthpiece. Anything more than this would cause division which would ultimately cause the entire house to fall. That's why in our church, anyone who would lead or serve must be "joined to me" by God. It is that critical. It also is the reason we have never had a major split in all the years of our ministry.

I thank God that I have elders around me who understand that whenever they receive detailed "bits and pieces" of the vision, then they have the freedom and the responsibility to "amplify" that which God is saying to me and then implement it. I have the confidence that my elders understand, first and foremost, they are God's gifts to me. They know they must catch the vision of the house to fulfill their calling. In our weekly elders' meetings, we spend our time finding the mind of God for our local church rather than arguing over everything the "mouthpiece" gives as direction from God.

I realize that this is a strong message and goes against the accepted "norm" for the Church, but I am confident that this is God's plan for Church leadership. I bear the scars of training, correction and submission on my heart and soul. These are my credentials of authority. I lead because I have learned to follow. Maybe by sharing a portion of my testimony you will be more able to understand what I'm trying to teach.

4
God's Pattern of Mentoring

I was saved and filled with the Spirit when I was eight years old, and immediately following my salvation, I had a very dramatic experience. During one of the rare times when no one was at home but me, I saw a ball of light suddenly appear in the hallway and begin to move into my bedroom. I knew it was God. The light entered the room and verbally called me into the ministry. I can still remember trying to tell my parents about it.

"Sure, Don. A ball of light appeared in the room ...sure!"

Over the next four years I had a number of unique, supernatural visitations, but I didn't tell anybody about them until years later, and then only to my wife for I had learned from the first time that I could not share everything God shared with me.

God "marked me" from a very early age. The youngest son of a preacher, I felt like I lived in the spotlight all the time. When I was 16, my older brother, Virgil, went away to college. Cynthia, my younger sister, was also going away, so I thought, "I'm not going to stay home either." I left Washington, DC., and went to Oklahoma City to attend prep school. I still remember those days as I thrived and became extremely independent, and I was proud that "I was my own man." Our society loves people who pull themselves up by their own boot-straps. We actually honor people who do not need others. God has a big problem with this attitude, but we just love it.

Nearing high school graduation, I made arrangements on my own to go to college on a full ride basketball scholarship (who said white men can't jump?!). Two weeks before school was scheduled to begin, Dad showed up. Even though I was my own man, my father was still my hero; he was my champion and model. I loved him very much, and we had a wonderful relationship during my teenage years. Dad told me he wanted me to read some information on Oral Roberts University in Tulsa, Oklahoma. I informed him I already had scholarship money to pay my tuition at the college I'd selected, thus saving him thousands of dollars, but Dad just said, "Read it."

Determining to continue "being my own man" and with college starting in only two weeks, I waited several days before I read the ORU literature. It said I had to have a certain grade point average (which I did not have), and I had to submit all of the application forms before their admissions deadline (which I had already missed), so I knew there was no way I would be accepted. When Dad came back, he asked if I had read the material and said, "You know, Don, I really feel that it might be the will of God for you to go to ORU." Soberly on the outside, but rejoicing on the inside, I told Dad there was no way they would accept me according to the literature he had given me. He looked at me and asked, "Would you believe it is God's will if you send it off and they accept you anyway?" Man, what a question, but two can play that game so I said, "Will you accept that it is not God's will if they reject it?"

With each of us agreeing on the terms, Dad once again left and I, being the great "man of faith" that I was, waited until just two or three days before I was to leave for college to send my stuff in. I could not believe it when I received a letter of acceptance from Oral Roberts University! God wanted me to go to a religious school. It would be a year later when I learned that Dad just called up some of his buddies and got me in. And I was thinking it was all God!

After spending two years at ORU, I decided I had had enough of the religious life, and I was going to see what the other side had to offer. While many people will tell you there is no "pleasure in sin" I can assure you that there is definitely pleasure in sin for a season and I wanted my season! The way I figured it, if you really wanted to sin "big time" then you needed to go to Hawaii to do it, so I got accepted to the University of Hawaii and made plans to "go sin." All I had to do was get past the three short months of summer break.

At home, the church was going through some major transitions. As part of this transitioning time, we had many conferences and services being conducted. At the conclusion of each service, the ministers would lay hands on people and prophesy over their lives. That didn't bother me. I just always made sure that I left the service before it was finished. God was not going to mess me up this time.

I almost made it. With only a few weeks left until I would be in Hawaii, suddenly, right in the middle of our praise and worship service one evening the speaker called me forward and asked me to kneel. Talk about "out of order!" Well, you can imagine what happened. All the ministers gathered around me and the Lord, through prophecy, disrupted my sinning spree as he literally apprehended me. All the plans I had made for my season of sin were shattered. I knew I was called to His ministry and there was no way of escape.

Since retreat was impossible, I decided negotiations were in order. I told God I would do anything He wanted me to do, and go anywhere He wanted me to go — anywhere that is except Evangel Church, and anything except coming under the authority of my father, my mother and my brother, Virgil. I didn't have a problem with anybody, it was just that "I was my own man; I was independent."

I no sooner said it than the voice of God said, "I want you to go to Evangel Church and come under the authority of your father and your mother." Thank God He didn't say Virgil!

A month had gone by when my dad came into my bedroom at a very ungodly hour to wake me up and say, "Donnie, Brother Jenkins has died." Brother Jenkins was a good man and served in the church as our janitor. With a look of fatherly love and tenderness, Dad said, "Don, I am just wondering if you would accept those responsibilities for a month or so until we can find somebody else?" Because Dad was being so sweet and kind, I said, "Sure, Dad, I would be glad to."

Well, a month became a year, and the year became five years. Five years! You have no idea how messy and dirty the people of God can be. Our church is 95 percent African American, and for five years this big, fat, white boy crawled in and out of those seats (don't forget that I have two years of college to help me!), and I picked up dumpster loads of paper, chewing gum, pumpkin seeds and occasionally even a chicken bone or two, all the while thinking, "You are really going places, Don. Yeah, you are really moving up the ladder. You have a great future."

You talk about "independence" days being over — I felt like everything about my life was being controlled by my father. In my mind, he determined not only what I was getting paid but my very status in life. One day I heard two guys in our church talking about me. They didn't see me or even know I was around. One asked, "What is Don Meares' ministry?" and the other one said, "He has the toilet bowl ministry!" I felt this deep grinding in my spirit. The toilet bowl ministry! Right.

Everything that used to be good in my relationship with my dad turned sour. We began to have major problems as I started seeing weaknesses in him and basically thought he was an idiot. The truth is that God was dealing with my rebellion; He was trying to teach me authority and submission, but at the time I just thought my dad was the problem.

I mentioned that I am fat. Do you know why I am so fat? From the age of 19 to 29, I lived a life of constant fasting. Nearly every year I would go on several 40-day fasts, and it destroyed my metabolism. Each time I went on a fast, I had only one request: Dear God, get me out of this church!

I was dying inside because everything that I thought God wanted me to do — preaching, teaching, radio, television — everything that was "ministry" in my eyes was not happening. Finally, with this continuing year after year, I got to the point where I was begging God as I fought depression, "Please God, get me out of here. I will do anything. I will go anywhere and do what You have called me to do. Just get me out of here!" I can assure you that if my mother had gotten her way, I'd have been out of there, for many times she "offered me the door," disgusted with my attitude and rebellion. Oh, how I wanted to go, but each time God would say, "No, this is where you are supposed to be."

Finally, after thirteen long years, during which no one even asked me to teach a class or do anything like what I considered ministry, I gave up. I quit trying to get it "my way." I reached a place in my life where all I could do was say, "God, I will never again ask You to let me preach or teach. I will never again ask You to let me do all those things that I thought You wanted me to do. I am completely dead to all of that. It's over and I give up. No more begging, weeping or asking from me." I literally died to myself.

In my death, I found myself praying, "God, here is what I am going to do if You'll bless it. Instead of the dreams and ambitions I have for my own ministry, I am going to live for that silver-haired old man. I am going to make that man look good. Anything he wants to do, I am going to make it happen. I'll leave everything I wanted to touch in ministry, and somehow, I am going to live my life through him." I wasn't just doing it for Dad, I was doing it for myself; and I meant it.

To my utter amazement, as I began to give myself to that man, I began to find a joy and fulfillment that I had not had for all those thirteen years of hell. Strange things began to happen. There were times when Dad would be preaching in a service and he would look down at me and say, "Prophesy," and I discovered I could prophesy word-for-word what was on his sermon notes, even though I had never seen them. I was being joined to my dad.

After years of dying and giving myself to my father and pastor, I got to a place where I literally "had the man's spirit." Somehow, God got it through my thick head that my destiny in ministry was tied to that man's ministry. This was very foreign to my way of thinking, for in this nation we are taught to be totally individualistic in all our concepts of ministry. Every man for himself, so to speak, when in reality the joy of ministry can only be attained as we connect to the ones whom God has destined us to become joined with. I finally understood that my destiny was tied to the destinies of my father and my brother, Virgil. I knew that God had joined us together, and I began to see how God had joined other men to us as well, and now our ministries were tied together.

In the process of catching my father's spirit, things began to happen in my life that I never dreamed possible. All of a sudden, a door for traveling ministry began to open to me. I now have so many requests for speaking engagements that I cannot accept them all, and I have never lifted a hand or made any effort to get them.

Today I am the senior pastor of our church. That's quite a leap from janitor and the toilet bowl ministry, isn't it? I never thought, dreamed or believed that it could have happened. My brother was trained for that position, but once I submitted to the will of God and to my family, then God moved both of us into our destined places of service. My brother receives me as his pastor today, and that is a testimony to his spiritual maturity and personal security in his calling. Everything that I could have desired has happened to me as a result of my acceptance of whom God joined me to and the abandonment of all my self wants.

This brings us to a place where we need to examine one of the great patterns of God from the Bible. Ed Cole is quoted as saying that every time God moves, He moves according to divine pattern or divine principle. Therefore, you and I must know the patterns and principles of Scripture in order to know the movements of God. While the New Testament is predominantly filled with God's principles and the Old Testament with the patterns, we can definitely see both of these patterns and principles throughout the entire Word of God.

One of those patterns that appears in both the Old and New Testaments is rarely taught anywhere, including in our seminaries. I'm speaking of the biblical pattern of mentoring, tutoring and joining. While most of us will readily admit that we desire the power of God for our lives and ministries, most of us would also have to admit that, more often than not, we feel quite powerless. That brings up an important question: Where did the leaders in Scripture get their power in God? The answer lies within the pattern of mentoring.

Joshua had power with God. One day he looked at the sun and said, "Stand still," and it did! I call that power. Joshua told the children of Israel that the walls of Jericho would fall if they obeyed God, and they fell. He conquered entire nations and possessed the Promised Land. Where did he get his power? What was his training process for ministry? What seminary did he go to?

If you study his life, you will discover that the one thing Joshua understood above all others was that he was called to serve Moses. Somehow, he knew that was God's will for his life. "I am to serve Moses...I am to wait on Moses... I am joined to Moses." However you want to say it, Joshua understood it and lived it.

When the entire nation of Israel chose to sin by worshipping the molten calf Aaron made while Moses was up on the mountain with God in Exodus 32, one man remained righteous besides Moses. That man was Joshua.

God warned Moses in Exodus 19:12-13 that no one was to pass the boundary of Mount Sinai. He said He would kill any man or beast that transgressed against Him, except for Moses and Aaron. So Moses told his young servant, Joshua, "I have to go up on the mountain because God wants to talk to me." From what we can gather from Scripture, Joshua's response was this: "I am joined to you. It's my job to wait on you and minister to you. If you go up the mountain, I go up the mountain. If God kills me, He kills me. I only know that I am not to leave your side."

In Exodus 32:17 when Moses turned to climb down the mountain with the tables of stone, we find Joshua waiting to meet him. He was there on the mountain waiting on Moses the whole time. As a result, he was the only man who had not participated in Israel's sin. You see, being joined to someone is not an infringement upon your identity and ministry. It is divine protection and a guarantee that you will accomplish all God has destined for you in this life, for what followed Joshua's meeting Moses was one of the most tragic scenes in the Bible.

Moses, upon entering the camp and learning of their great sin, challenged the people with the question, "Who is on the Lord's side?" Then he ordered the sons of Levi to destroy those who failed to cross the line. It is almost certain that a number of the original seventy elders who had prophesied only forty days before were in the group of 3,000 that were slain.

When the time came for Israel's next leader to step into place, God told Moses to lay his hands on Joshua and God said,

> **Cause him to stand before Eleazar the priest and all the congregation, and you shall commission him in their sight.**
>
> **You shall invest him with some of your authority.**
> **Numbers 27:19-20 RSV**

The question we must answer is why was Joshua chosen instead of Aaron the high priest or Caleb the other spy who, like Joshua, delivered the faithful report about the Promised Land? The answer is simple. Joshua had Moses' spirit. He met God's requirements to be the next leader. He paid the price.

The story of Elisha and Elijah also follows God's pattern of joining. How does God train a young prophet to take over a prophetic mantle?

"Wash my hands, son. Carry my case."

"But when will we get into the Bible studies?"

"That comes later. The important stuff is happening right now."

That is the whole process of training, for until we learn to serve with total joy we will never be able to lead from God's perspective. Elijah, the older prophet, did everything he could to sever the relationship with Elisha as his own homegoing drew near, but Elisha passed his "final exam," for the one thing the younger prophet understood was, "I will not allow myself to be separated from you until it has to be. I am joined to you to serve you." Sure enough, upon Elijah being taken by God, Elisha began to move in an extraordinary anointing and mantle. Why? Because he received a double portion of "the spirit of Elijah."

Does this pattern continue? Oh, yes. Where did the Apostle Paul get his power and authority? We know that he had a tremendous conversion experience on the road to Damascus. He was a trained scholar who could speak a lot of languages, and he had been trained in the Jewish religion all of his life. Even before his conversion, he was a man to be reckoned with. Now that he was saved, he decided to go to Jerusalem to sit down with the "big boys," but the big boys wouldn't give him an audience.

Paul was determined to serve Jesus, so he just started preaching. Educated or not, he was a complete novice in the gospel so he caused great problems in the city. I love the passage that describes how the Grecian Jews tried to kill Saul, and after the brethren shipped him out of Jerusalem to Tarsus, it says, **Then had the churches rest...** (Acts 9:29-31). This highly educated and motivated seminarian fled to the desert. He was depressed and frustrated. No one seemed to recognize what God did for him. What was their problem?

Finally, a prophet from Antioch sought out Paul and took him to Antioch where he evidently submitted himself to the church there. Within a few verses, he was sent as a companion to Barnabas to help the persecuted church in Jerusalem where they witnessed the miraculous deliverance of Peter from Herod's prison. (Acts 11:30-12:25.) None of these things would have happened unless an apostle named Barnabas had said, "I see something in Paul," and went out of his way to seek him out in Tarsus (Acts 11:25-26).

Eventually, in Acts 13:1 , a group of anointed prophets and teachers got together to fast and pray. Then the Holy Spirit said, **Separate me Barnabas and Saul for the work**

whereunto I have called them (Acts 13:2). The order of the names is extremely important. Notice that Saul is not in charge. "First mention" is an important key of interpretation. Barnabas is clearly the leader, but the interesting thing is that before the first missionary journey was over, the order had changed! In Acts 13:9, Saul's name is permanently changed from Saul (which means destroyer) to Paul (which means worker). After Paul publicly confronted a sorcerer in power and authority, verse 13 changes the order of mention and says, **Now when Paul and his company loosed from Paphos...** (Acts 13:13), and by the time Paul has ended his address to a Jewish synagogue in Antioch, the writer of the Book of Acts has permanently changed the order of mention to **Paul and Barnabas** (Acts 13:43). Paul had learned everything God desired from the man He sent to mentor him. This was fortunate because a major division came between Barnabas and Paul over a young man named John Mark. These two great church leaders actually ended up dividing their joining in God over this young man, and it is interesting to note that this is the last we hear of Barnabas in the Bible. It is even more interesting that later in his ministry, it was Paul who trained John Mark for his ministry.

Another young man Paul trained to move in might and power was Timothy. In fact, Paul wrote some amazing things about him:

> **But I trust in the Lord Jesus to send Timotheus shortly unto you, that I also may be of good comfort, when I know your state.**
>
> **For I have no man like-minded, who will naturally care for your state.**
>
> **For all seek their own, not the things that are Jesus Christ's.**
>
> **But ye know the proof of him, that, as a son with the father, he hath served with me in the gospel.**
>
> **Philippians 2:19-22**

Paul had fathered the church at Corinth, and when they got big-headed, they basically told Paul, "Who do you think you are? You're really not very eloquent in speech, and you don't have much demonstration in power. We have some other guys now who are coming to the church and we really like them better, like Apollos."

Who did Paul send to straighten out the church? Timothy. Timothy had spiritual power and authority because he was "joined" to Paul like a son to a father. Paul said he had no one in the ministry like Timothy. And Timothy had the goods, because he straightened out the mess at Corinth!

Of all the "joining" and "mentoring" examples in the New Testament, I believe one of the greatest to be of Jesus with the twelve disciples, and within that company of twelve Jesus definitely had three that were closer to Him than all the rest. Now you may not like my saying that, but it's the truth; and Jesus made no apology to the twelve when He wanted to share some very special things with Peter, James and John. He simply told the nine to stay and the three to come. Of them all, Peter was probably the smartest of the twelve because he learned a lesson that most Christians never understand: The greatest things you learn in God can come by what you do wrong as well as by what you do right.

We cannot receive God's wisdom outside of correction and instruction, and Peter did not mind being corrected. Every time Jesus asked the disciples a question, everybody just waited for Peter to stick his foot in his mouth. Peter didn't care if he looked like a fool because he wanted to learn. But think about it: Who stood up and preached a sermon that brought thousands to Christ on the Day of Pentecost? Who walked in such faith and power that people were literally healed when his shadow fell on them? Who walked on the water while his companions cowered in a boat? Who is the one who learned more than the others? It was Peter, because he understood that wisdom comes by learning from what you do wrong more than what you do right.

One of the greatest mistakes made by pastors and leaders in the Church (both on the national and local level), is that when they make mistakes (and we all do) they never let the people know about it. I think it's healthy for a congregation to know their pastor makes mistakes and learns from them. This encourages all the rest of us that there is still some hope and maybe God isn't through with us yet.

I praise God for Bible passages telling how Paul went through a city thanking God, when the Holy Spirit suddenly interrupted to ask, "What are you doing here, son?" When Paul explained that he was going to preach and get people saved, the Spirit basically said, "No. I do not want you here," so Paul went somewhere else. He was the great apostle of God, and he still missed it once in a while. Thank God we have passages like that. It encourages me when I read about all the Bible leaders who blew it. I realize that there is still hope for me.

That brings us to a very important aspect of this discussion. It's one thing to make a mistake and learn from it, but is it possible to make so many mistakes that we miss our intended destiny? I believe that the Bible overwhelmingly teaches that it is.

Moses, I believe, did not fulfill his total purpose and destiny in God. Called by God to lead the children of Israel out of Egypt and bondage, Moses was destined to also lead them into their possession of the Promised Land. At one point in that journey, God was so fed up with the people that He told Moses to step aside so He could kill his rebellious subjects while at the same time promising to raise up a new nation from the descendants of Moses. The people were saved only because Moses interceded for them.

I have discovered that if God wants to do something, He will usually do it no matter what we do, because He is always right in what He wants to do. Moses delayed the death of his generation, but God killed those people anyway. "All right, Moses, I won't kill them now. I'll just let those hard-headed rebels walk around in circles for forty years until they drop dead."

I think Moses missed it when he intervened with God's desire through his intercession, because those people ultimately rejected their own Promised Land through unbelief. Moses walked with them through those forty years in the desert because he had become joined to them. The relationships of flesh that Moses cared so much about ultimately influenced him to be rejected by God. Once God's leaders reach certain levels of maturity, God does not allow them much latitude for double-mindedness. Yes, Moses was still a great man of God and one of Israel's greatest leaders. He met Jesus Christ with Elijah on the mount of transfiguration, and was finally allowed to step onto the soil of the Promised Land in the presence of the Messiah — but — He never fulfilled his destiny of taking the people of God into their rightful possession of that land.

I believe another man who missed his total destiny was Jonathan, the friend of David. The joining of Jonathan and David was so strong that the Bible declares their love was greater than the love of a man for a woman. They cut a covenant with each other that was supposed to be forever. At the time Jonathan and David were joined to each other, Jonathan was still the heir apparent to the throne of Israel. He was going to be the next king. And yet Jonathan, because he was joined to David, understood that somehow David was to be the next king. (1 Samuel 23:17.) He knew that in their friendship and later in Israel, David would be the ruler, and Jonathan had no problem with that.

Jonathan had one of the greatest destinies a young man could ever have, yet his story is one of the most tragic in the Bible. He was destined to be a part of the greatest Old Testament kingdom which would be led by David, yet for some reason Jonathan died a premature death. Why? What happened that so altered Jonathan's destiny?

In the natural, Jonathan was joined to the house of Saul, the "house of flesh" that God had rejected. In the Spirit he was also joined to David, the man after God's own heart, the "spiritual house." Jonathan's rich destiny and purpose was in God, but because he would not sever his joining to the "house of flesh," Jonathan missed his destiny in God. That is a tragedy.

Have you noticed that there are certain sayings of Jesus that most preachers just don't preach or teach anymore? He said some hard things like,

> Think not that I am come to send peace on earth: I came not to send peace, but a sword.
>
> For I am come to set a man at variance against his father, and the daughter against her mother, and the daughter in law against her mother in law.
>
> And a man's foes shall be they of his own household.
>
> **Matthew 10:34-36**

When the purposes of God brought a sword to his household, Jonathan would not sever the natural joining that was in direct rebellion against God. He ended up dying beside his rebellious father instead of reigning beside his righteous friend, thus missing his whole purpose in life.

It is extremely interesting to notice who God used in David's life as his mentor. Unlike Saul, who had Samuel the prophet and priest of God to train him, God used Saul to train David. Now, I'm not suggesting that David was joined to Saul, but I do believe that God put David under Saul's authority so that David could learn from Saul's horrendous mistakes how to rule in righteousness. He must have learned well, for when Absalom, David's son, led a coup against him to win the kingdom, David just left the palace and even let an old man throw rocks and dirt on him while cursing him. Though David's generals wanted to kill the man, David told them not to touch him. David's wisdom was rooted in remembering the wrong way to rule.

By now I'm sure you're wondering where I'm going in all of this. Well, believe it or not, all of this applies directly to church elders, deacons and leaders. In order to be effective as a leader and successful in attaining your purpose in God, you must know who you are serving, and for that to be attained, you must know to whom you are joined.

Let's go back to a question I asked you at the beginning of this chapter. Who did Jesus serve? Surely, by now, we have established that it was not the people. So, whom did He serve?

> **Believest thou not that I am in the Father, and the Father in me? The words that I speak unto you I speak not of myself: but the Father that dwelleth in me, he doeth the works.**
>
> **John 14:10**
>
> **Then said Jesus unto them, When ye have lifted up the Son of man, then shall ye know that I am he, and that I do nothing of myself; but as my Father hath taught me, I speak these things.**
>
> **And he that sent me is with me: the Father hath not left me alone; for I do always those things that please him.**
>
> **John 8:28-29**
>
> **Have I been so long time with you, and yet hast thou not known me, Philip? he that hath seen me hath**

seen the Father; and how sayest thou then, Shew us the Father?

John 14:9

The whole key to the effective ministry of Jesus Christ was that He served only the Father. No one else. Jesus' entire life was dedicated to serving, pleasing and accomplishing the will of the Father. If the Father told Him to heal only one man at the pool of Bethesda, then that man is the only one He healed. The success of His mission depended totally on His complete obedience to God's plan, even down to such minute details as requesting the sour wine on the cross. Jesus totally died to all of His desires and ambitions, and the Father was living His life through Him. Long before Calvary, Jesus had crucified Himself in order to allow the Father to live.

Why do you think He spent so many nights in prayer? He was determined to hear what the Father wanted Him to do the next day. He was fully God, but He was also a man Who had to hear God the same way you and I have to hear Him. Jesus was successful because He was determined to carry out His Father's instructions — nothing more and nothing less. Jesus served the Father (not just the people or their needs and wants) by seeing what happened in heaven and bringing it down to earth.

I should point out that while Jesus directly obeyed the will of the Father at all times, He still had human teachers that the Father utilized in His life to train Him for the Father's purpose. First, He submitted to His parents and the spiritual authorities in the synagogues and in the temple of Herod. He also submitted to the laws and the Roman authorities and would even teach later to "render unto Caesar the things that are Caesar's and unto God the things that are God's."

Throughout His lifetime, Jesus submitted to those shepherds who had lived on the earth years before and spoken prophetically of the Messiah Who would come. Jesus Christ literally fulfilled thousands of ancient prophecies, scriptural types and shadows, and Jewish rabbinical traditions during His life on earth. If He had failed in any of these, He would not have qualified as the true Messiah, because God is a God of order.

Many Christians find this hard to believe, because they think it is logical that the only human shepherds Jesus could have would be the same group of hypocritical religious leaders that He constantly argued with. He did submit to the religious leaders in authority where they followed the Word and authority of God. He only confronted them where they were in outright sin and rebellion against the true will of God. That is why He told His disciples,

> **The scribes and the Pharisees sit in Moses' seat:**
>
> **All therefore whatsoever they bid you observe, that observe and do; but do not ye after their works: for they say, and do not.**
>
> **Matthew 23:2-3**

Jesus' submission to the ancient prophetic shepherds in Scripture is revealed at the River Jordan when He was with John the Baptist. When Jesus asked John to baptize Him, John said he couldn't, but Jesus said he had to, **For thus it becometh us to fulfill all righteousness** (Matthew 3:15). Jesus was telling John, "I know what the shepherds told Me to do. I know I have to fulfill every jot and tittle of My Father's Word. I must fulfill everything that has come out of His servants' mouths. I have to do it."

When Jesus was on the cross, nearly suffocated, and weak from continuous loss of blood, He asked for a drink. The gospel of John says He asked for the drink **that the scripture might be fulfilled,** knowing that He would receive an undrinkable mixture of sour wine and gall. (John 19:28.) Jesus knew He had to do it. Why? King David, one of His prophetic shepherds, prophesied by the Holy Ghost 28 generations before the Lord's birth, **They gave me also gall for my meat; and in my thirst they gave me vinegar to drink** (Psalm 69:21). Much of our Lord's guidance and direction in life came from these shepherds.

It is no coincidence that people wondered if Jesus was actually the revived presence of the prophets Jeremiah or Isaiah. There was something about His ministry that made them think of the miraculous ministries of these powerful prophets.

The point being that even Jesus Christ submitted to the authority and input of shepherds and mentors and thereby took on a measure of their anointing and ministry that was recognizable to the people.

Speaking of that, we have already looked at the ministries of Moses and Joshua, Elijah and Elisha, and I've even described what happened in my life, but one of the most interesting impartations of power we can study took place in the life of David.

In your study of the Bible, have you ever read about David's mighty men? These were some strange dudes. One of them was walking on a path when he looked down and saw a lion in a pit. He said to himself, "I don't have anything to do, and it's not quite lunch time, so I think I'll go down and play with the lion and see if I can kill it." (See 2 Samuel 23:20.) Now that is the mentality of a strange person!

Another one of these 400 mighty men had a particular fondness of lentils, a type of bean. I'm not sure anyone understands why or how it happened, but when a Philistine army squadron attacked a force of Israelite soldiers, everyone ran away — everyone except Shammah. This man refused to leave his bean patch like a normal man would do. (2 Samuel 23:11-12.) Shammah took his stand in the middle of his bean patch and said, "Nobody but nobody takes my beans. I love my beans." Then this food lover began to fight the entire band of attackers single-handedly over a batch of beans! Now even in our day, this is a strange person, but evidently he wasn't the only one that day. As Shammah proceeded to kill these attackers one by one with an amazing anointing and ability, the men who were after his beans didn't have sense enough to run! I guess they had formed a circle around him and the guys in the back were pushing forward to see what was happening with the bean freak. "Let me see this guy...Man, is he strange." Meanwhile, this mighty bean lover was saying, "I love my beans. I will fight for my beans to the death. I warned you...!"

When it was all over, there were dead bodies scattered all around the man's beloved bean patch, and Shammah had become one of "the three," the three greatest fighters in David's troop of 400 men. Since these warriors were ranked strictly by their bravery and exploits of war, Shammah must have killed between 300 and 800 men that day, because the warrior ranked below him killed 300 men single-handedly with a spear — and he was on the "second string." (2 Samuel 23:11-12,18-19.)

As humorous as this story is, my point is this: How did a group of misfits hiding in a cave turn into such a band of renowned soldiers?

First Samuel 22 describes the kind of men David discovered in the cave at Adullam. These men ended up as Old Testament equivalents of "superheroes," but look at what they were before they joined up with David. The Bible says they were distressed, discontented, depressed, in debt and down and out. They were the scum of the earth, they were considered outlaws at best and nobodies most of the time. Four hundred of these society rejects lived together in that cave. David walked into that cave, and when he came out, he was the captain of the band. Now I know a lot of us think that David was a small, frail boy who was always skipping with a harp in his hand, singing songs and praising God all the time, and maybe practicing a little with a slingshot, but I believe we are missing something about David's nature. The Bible says he was "a bloody man of war."

This is the man who killed 1,000 men to win the hand of Saul's daughter. He obviously didn't stop his warfare training with his victory over Goliath. David was such a deadly warrior that the women of the day used to sing and chant, "Saul has killed this thousands, but David has slain ten thousands."

David bolted into the cave at Adullam, dogged by 3,000 soldiers with orders from King Saul to kill him on sight. David looked at the rag-tag bunch of losers and said, "If anybody wants to follow me, follow me. I'm taking over." Those men had nothing to lose, so they joined the man of God. From the moment they made that decision, they began to experience a miraculous transformation.

These losers were shocked the first time they entered a battle with David. They not only won the battle, but they completely destroyed the Philistine invaders; and then the adventure really began. These guys discovered they had changed; they were awesome in battle. They didn't have any modern weapons, but they were unmatched in battle even when they were grossly outnumbered. Where did they get their power? What changed them? Here is the answer. When they went to war, because they were joined to David, the anointed of the Lord, they began to war under David's spirit and anointing. This David who as a young boy killed the bear, the lion, and the giant Goliath literally imparted his spirit to these men because they chose to join themselves to David. Just like him, they became bloody men of war with a mandate to defend their captain — they had his spirit, and because of that, they refused to live anywhere that was not close to where David was.

Let me challenge your thinking with a fascinating exhortation — especially if you are a pastor or church leader in ministry. What would your church or ministry be like if you had fifty people who had your spirit? What could you accomplish for Jesus if you had some "faithful men" to undergird you at all times? Do you know why David had the greatest kingdom in the Bible? He had 400 men who had his spirit! These guys would do anything for David, because their destiny was directly linked to his. If David looked good, they looked good. If David felt good, they felt good. If David was fulfilled, they were fulfilled. Though they were each individually their own person, corporately their destiny and vision was directly joined to David and without him they would have been nothing but a bunch of losers.

The desire these men had to minister for and with David is greatly underscored for us as we view David taking a break during a particular battle and muttering to himself, **Oh that one would give me drink of the water of the well of Bethlehem** (2 Samuel 23:15). The Bible tells us "the three mighty men" overheard his whispered wish, and they risked their lives to break through enemy lines to get their captain a drink of water from that well which was right in the middle of the enemy camp!

What would happen if all you or your pastor had to do was to whisper something, and it happened in your church? Can you begin to see how powerful "joining" is for both the leader and the church? There is absolutely nothing we cannot accomplish for God if we work together with those whom God has joined us to. This won't happen, however, until we begin to teach and practice mentoring, tutoring and joining.

As a senior pastor, I dream a lot about Joshua 1:18, where God had touched the hearts of two-and-one-half tribes of Israel who said to Joshua, "Look, you do not have to ask us nor do you have to beg us to do something for you. Simply command us, and we will do whatever you say. And if anybody in the camp will not do what you have commanded, we will kill them!" Brother, there was no rebellion in this house. The destiny of God for Israel ruled supreme.

We must begin in all our local churches and ministries to have men and women just like those described above if we truly plan to see God's destiny come to pass in our lives and churches. The Scriptures provide clear patterns to help us train men and women for ministry in the church. Where we miss it is in believing that we are called to do something by ourselves rather than understanding God's desire for joining so that we can catch the spirit and vision of our leader and thereby accomplish all that the Holy Spirit has put within their heart to do. For those who are faithful and obedient in being joined with their leader, the day will come when they will enter their own destiny with a "double anointing," because they will minister with both their own anointing from God and with the imparted anointing of the one they served and were joined to.

If you are a pastor reading this book, let me be quick to say that not everyone in your church has to have your spirit, but I definitely believe that the elders of a church can never accomplish what God has called them to do unless they have the spirit of the presiding elder in the house. God clearly imparts His vision for the house to one person in any local church. The reason is pretty obvious. Anything with more than one head is a freak, and anything with more than one vision has division. Unity among the elders is essential for the fulfillment of God's plan to come to pass for His local church.

If you are a church elder reading this book, please know that you can only be effective and flow in God's blessing when you realize that you are a gift to the man or woman of

God who He has established as the head of your house. Your job is not only to catch the leader's vision, but to implement it. Likewise, if you are a deacon reading this book, you must understand that your major call is to carefully watch what is happening to the leadership of a church so that you can instantly spot anything that might come up which would distract your leadership from their responsibility to lead. As a deacon, you should have the heart and the authority to take care of whatever it is so your leader can continue to seek the Lord and establish His work in your church.

I pray that every leader in the church will learn how to mentor and tutor those whom God joins to them. I further pray that every believer will be open to obey God's leading when He desires to join them to a servant of God. This is simply His way of equipping the saints for the work of the ministry and moving all of us further along in His corporate destiny for our lives.

5

The Necessity of Corporate Unity

Would you agree with me that some things in life are absolutely amazing? I don't know about you, but as I travel across this nation and around the world, I am privileged to see some pretty amazing things. Some are architectural wonders while others are simply awesome displays of God's creative powers in this earth. Would you like to know, though, what amazes me the most with regard to the local church and the Church universal? It is the lack of understanding that the people of God have with regard to how very important unity is to the plan of God and their destinies in Him. To watch how most Christians live, they must believe that they are the only son or daughter that God has because they live their lives as though no one else were involved.

Have you ever considered how very important unity is to God and His divine purpose for your life? According to my Bible, it is only when the people of God are in one accord that anything worthwhile happens in their lives. Time and again the Scriptures teach that it is only through unity that God blesses and expands His kingdom in this earth and in our lives. With that being true, what do you believe about unity — especially unity within your local assembly?

In writing to the church at Ephesus, Paul sent a powerful message regarding the importance of unity. To appreciate all that he said, however, we must understand that he was not writing to one individual but rather to the entire family of God.

I, therefore, the prisoner of the Lord, entreat you to walk in a manner worthy of the calling with which you have been called,

With all humility and gentleness, with patience, showing forbearance to one another in love,

Being diligent to preserve the unity of the Spirit in the bond of peace.

There is one body and one Spirit, just as also you were called in one hope of your calling;

One Lord, one faith, one baptism,

One God and Father of all who is over all and through all and in all.

But to each one of us grace was given according to the measure of Christ's gift.

Therefore it says, "When He ascended on high, He led captive a host of captives, and He gave gifts to men."

(Now this expression, "He ascended," what does it mean except that He also had descended into the lower parts of the earth?

He who descended is Himself also He who ascended far above all the heavens, that He might fill all things.)

And He gave some as apostles, and some as prophets, and some as evangelists, and some as pastors and teachers,

For the equipping of the saints for the work of service, to the building up of the body of Christ;

Until we all attain to the unity of the faith, and of the knowledge of the Son of God, to a mature man, to the measure of the stature which belongs to the fullness of Christ.

Ephesians 4:1-13 NASB

What a tremendous revelation the Apostle Paul gives the Ephesians. Everything they desire to do in and for God must be preserved and perfected in unity. His admonition to preserve the "unity of the Spirit" is the challenge that will ultimately allow them to achieve "unity in the faith."

"So, how does that work," you might be asking? What does it mean to "preserve the unity of the Spirit"? Does that mean we must agree with each other on every point of our church doctrine? No, it doesn't. Well, does it mean that we have to agree on everything concerning the Bible? No, that's not necessary either. Maintaining unity of the Spirit means that we must come into an attitude where we are in one accord, one heart, and one mind with each other with our relationship being founded upon the lordship of Jesus Christ in our lives. I don't have to agree with every doctrine you believe in order to preserve the unity of the Spirit, but I must be able to discern you are a believer and accept you as a brother or sister based on our being related as family through Christ.

The key to understanding what I'm going to teach you in this chapter is wrapped up in that one word — family. Whether we recognize it or not, Jesus Christ came to reconcile us back to God the Father so that His family would be intact. God is a family God. He thinks in terms of family, and He responds to us based on what every member of the family does — not just what we do individually.

This is where most of us miss it. If I were to ask you if you believed we were all a part of "the family of God," I'm sure most of you would respond in the affirmative. However, if you will listen to yourself when you pray, you probably pray like about 90 percent of the body of Christ — as if you were the only son or daughter God has! "God, I can't help what Susie or Johnny is doing, but God, please bless me because I've been very, very good. Amen." Then when your prayers aren't answered the way you believe they should have been, you question why God is being so mean to you. Maybe the problem is not you — maybe it's Susie or Johnny!

Now, I realize that I've just dropped yet another "bombshell" on some of our religious thinking, but folks, the truth of the matter is that God is a family God, and just like our families in the natural, what every member of the family does affects all the rest. I am convinced that the reason many in the church are sick, destitute and dying is because there is disunity within their local "families" and therefore their own prayers and blessings are being hindered.

"Now, wait a minute, Brother Don. I've been with you up until now, but this is just too much! I mean, where in the Bible can you substantiate such a ridiculous idea?" I'm really glad you asked that question. Let's look in the book of Joshua just after the walls of Jericho had fallen.

(In order to understand the scripture and get the full impact of how very important unity is, I need to "fill in the blanks" so, as Paul Harvey says, you'll know "the rest of the story.")

Joshua has successfully led the children of Israel around Jericho for the seven days as commanded by God, and just as was promised, the walls fell down and Israel conquered Jericho and possessed the city. In taking the city, however, the Lord spoke to Joshua to place the city under a ban which forbade the Israelites to take any of the spoils. Everything in the city that was not destroyed was to be given to God and God alone. (See Joshua 6:17-19.) Now, with that understanding, let's begin reading in chapter seven of Joshua.

> **But the sons of Israel acted unfaithfully in regard to the things under the ban, for Achan, the son of Carmi, the son of Zabdi, the son of Zerah, from the tribe of Judah, took some of the things under the ban, therefore the anger of the Lord burned against the sons of Israel.**
> **Joshua 7:1 NASB**

What is this? How can God hold all the sons of Israel accountable for what only one person did? The scripture here says that Achan is the one who took the stuff. Why is God mad at everybody?

To fully understand this, we are once again going to have to look at a principle of God that up until now we have just alluded to, and that is the fact that God does not think like we think. His ways and methods are much stricter than ours, and He holds everyone accountable to His ways and means.

> **For my thoughts are not your thoughts, neither are your ways my ways, saith the Lord.**
>
> **For as the heavens are higher than the earth, so are my ways higher than your ways, and my thoughts than your thoughts.**
>
> Isaiah 55:8-9

See, God just doesn't think like you and I think. I know that seems unfair, but it's the way it is. God is a family God and He thinks in terms of family when He deals with us. Look at this passage again closely. Who actually committed the transgression? Achan, right? Okay. Who did God hold accountable for the sin and get mad at? Achan? Nope. All the sons of Israel. You see, that's how important unity is to God. If one messes up, it's as though the entire group messed up. Why? Because we are joined to each other and therefore are responsible one for another. I know. You don't like that, do you? I don't blame you. I don't particularly care for this concept myself, but I have come to understand that whether I like it or not — that's the way it is — and, if I want to see the blessing of God in our local church, then I must be willing to walk in God's desire for unity. I'll share with you later in this chapter what that means to me as a pastor. Right now, though, let's get back to our story in Joshua chapter seven.

Joshua has no idea that God is mad at Israel. All he knows is that Jericho was a tremendous victory and they are well on their way to possessing the Promised Land. As he turns his attention to the next place of battle, he decides that they will take the small town of Ai. Because it was so tiny, however, the leadership decided that only two or three thousand men at the most would be needed to completely conquer the inhabitants. Watch what happens.

> Now Joshua sent men from Jericho to Ai, which is near Beth-aven, east of Bethel, and said to them, "Go up and spy out the land." So the men went up and spied out Ai.
>
> And they returned to Joshua and said to him, "Do not let all the people go up; only about two or three thousand men need go up to Ai; do not make all the people toil up there, for they are few."
>
> So about three thousand men from the people went up there, but they fled from the men of Ai.
>
> And the men of Ai struck down about thirty-six of their men, and pursued them from the gate as far as Shebarim, and struck them down on the descent, so the hearts of the people melted and became as water.
>
> Then Joshua tore his clothes and fell to the earth on his face before the ark of the Lord until the evening, both he and the elders of Israel; and they put dust on their heads.
>
> And Joshua said, "Alas, O Lord God, why didst Thou ever bring this people over the Jordan, only to deliver us into the hand of the Amorites, to destroy us? If only we had been willing to dwell beyond the Jordan!
>
> "Oh, Lord, what can I say since Israel has turned their back before their enemies?
>
> "For the Canaanites and all the inhabitants of the land will hear of it, and they will surround us and cut off our name from the earth. And what wilt Thou do for Thy great name?"
>
> So the Lord said to Joshua, "Rise up! Why is it that you have fallen on your face?
>
> "Israel has sinned, and they have also transgressed My covenant which I commanded them. And they have

**even taken some of the things under the ban and have
both stolen and deceived. Moreover, they have also put
them among their own things.**

**"Therefore the sons of Israel cannot stand before
their enemies; they turn their backs before their
enemies, for they have become accursed. I will not be
with you any more unless you destroy the things under
the ban from your midst."**

Joshua 7:2-12 NASB

If you're like me, you just want to shake your head as
you read this account. How could God hold everybody
accountable for what only one person did? The answer is
simple. God does not think like you and I think. In our
democracy where we live, we are raised to let every person
be accountable for his or her own actions. The penalty for
"missing it" falls upon the one who erred. With God,
however, it's not always that way. While it's true each
individual must give an account to God for their own
personal lives and choices, it is also true that each corporate
body must give an account to God for how they functioned
together as a family. Just as surely as we have individual
and corporate destinies, we also have individual and
corporate accountabilities. When you or I do something (or
don't do something) that God has spoken for our entire
body, then the entire body will suffer from our
disobedience. This, in a nutshell, is the reason why so many
of our churches are in trouble today. It's not that everyone is
missing it, but by not dealing with the ones who are, we
reap upon the entire church the discipline which God must
give in order to reach and restore the rebels.

You see, God commanded all of Israel to abide by the
ban placed upon Jericho. The fact that only Achan
disobeyed did not excuse the rest of Israel in God's eyes.
Why? Because at this point in time God is dealing with the
entire nation as one — not as individuals. You may be
thinking, "But that's not fair." It's not a matter of being
"fair," it's just the way God thinks. His ways are higher

than ours and He isn't going to change. When He chooses to deal with the entire body as "one" then the entire body has to do what is being commanded. If they don't then the entire body will suffer for it.

Poor Joshua. He didn't have a clue as to what was wrong. Jericho was such a tremendous success against insurmountable odds, and now Israel has just been dealt a major defeat, not to mention the loss of 36 lives, over a little "no-nothing" town called Ai. For all practical purposes, Israel should have defeated these guys in their sleep, but instead they turned and ran away from them losing 36 of their men in the process.

Joshua did what any good shepherd will do in a crisis: He prayed. "God, what's going on? How could this have happened? What have we done to displease You so?" And, as he was praying the Lord spoke sternly to him telling him to get up and shut up! The problem, God informed him, was that Israel went against His ban on Jericho and even took some of the spoils into their tents. Even though only one person was actually responsible for the sin, God held all of Israel accountable just as though they had all done it.

I can hear Joshua now, "But Lord, I did what I was supposed to do. I walked around the city — even though I didn't really want to. But, I did. I walked around it just like You told me to. I jumped up and down and shouted when I was supposed to, and after we finished — I left. I didn't touch a thing! So don't say, God, that I have sinned and that I have touched the accursed thing, because I didn't do it. Do you understand that, God? I DIDN'T DO IT!"

Unfortunately for Joshua, his appeal didn't change a thing. As far as God was concerned the whole nation was guilty and until they dealt with the person responsible, they were all under the punishment for his disobedience. In short, God said He was through with them! No more blessings, no more miracles, no more victories until the sin was dealt with. WOW!

If you think Joshua had a hard time with this, I wonder how the rest of Israel handled it — especially the widows of the 36 men who were killed because of Achan's disobedience? Can you imagine having to answer those widow's questions? "Why, Joshua? Why were our spouses killed?" His response would have had to be, "Because they sinned. God said that's why we were defeated by Ai and that's why your spouses died. They sinned."

There's no doubt in my mind that these women objected loudly and at great length, informing Joshua that their husbands had certainly not sinned. "Just come over to our tents and see for yourself," I'm sure was one of the things they said, but alas, Joshua could only reinforce what he had already told them. God said that all the sons of Israel had sinned and therefore God's hand had lifted off Israel and His blessing would not be restored until the accursed things were destroyed.

From this we learn a very important lesson. Our actions affect far more than ourselves if we are truly a part of a local body. Since we are joined together as one, then our obedience will bless the entire body while our disobedience will hinder the body. Only in walking together in the "unity of the Spirit" will we be able to successfully accomplish all that God desires for us to do corporately.

Now the task fell to Joshua to find the "accursed thing," because God said, **... I will not be with you any more unless you destroy the things under the ban from your midst** (Joshua 7:12 NASB). In other words, no amount of prayer and fasting was going to get God's blessing back for Israel. This is so foreign to us, isn't it? Most of us have never been taught it is possible to face a defeat or crisis that can't be prayed away because of something that somebody else has done in the church. We have been taught to believe that as long as we take care of "number one" then God will deal with everyone else individually, but here we see that our teaching has been in error. When it comes to a corporate body of believers, and when God speaks a word for the entire body to walk in, then one person or 100 persons disobeying that word brings the same results — failure to do and become what God has decreed for our body.

So, what do we do about it? Well, we have to do what Joshua did. We have to root out the problem and deal with the sin before the blessing of God will be restored. But, here's the "kicker." Our job is not to personally "seek out and destroy" but rather to seek God's face until He reveals the problem Himself. How do you know that, Brother Don? Because that's exactly what God told Joshua to do.

In Joshua 7:13-15, the Lord commanded Joshua to have the people consecrate themselves and then to present themselves unto the Lord as a whole nation. Then, by casting lots, the Spirit of God revealed where the problem was rooted, beginning with the tribe, then the clans, then the families and finally to the one individual responsible for all of Israel to be under God's wrath. Talk about an awesome God.

Out of an estimated "church" of three million people, God revealed the one individual who was causing the problem for the entire three million! As the final lot was cast, Achan was revealed as the "one in a million" who was guilty of disobeying God's command for His people, and though Achan confessed to coveting and stealing a Babylonian garment and some silver and gold, it was too late. His willful sin had doomed him, his wife, and his family. But his sin had also cost 36 men their lives, depriving 36 families of their husbands, fathers and providers. In fact, it almost caused a nation of three million people to be cursed! Why? Because when God speaks a command for His entire body to obey, then one person's disobedience will hinder the rest of the body from becoming all God desires for them to become. Like it or not, we are family and we are joined one to another. Unity is not just a good idea, it is imperative in order to become, as a church, all the Lord has destined for us to become.

By now, I imagine you are thinking several things. First, you might be thinking, "Well, that's impossible. There's no way we can always agree on everything." You're absolutely right if you mean we can't always agree on specific doctrinal issues. "Unity of the faith" is a process that can only come about as we strive to preserve "the unity of the Spirit" which is based solely on our relationship to each other in Christ. As a people, we are as diverse as the flakes of snow that fall from the sky. No two flakes are ever exactly alike. However, when they fall to the ground and join together, they become a beautiful "blanket" that covers the earth and seemingly are exactly alike. That's the way it is with a local church. No two people will be alike or think alike. We have been redeemed from every race, kindred and nation on this planet. Our backgrounds and upbringings are as different as the proverbial "night and day" analogies, but we can be united in His lordship. Because of His blood we can be one in the Spirit, and as we walk together in this covenant we will attain the unity of the faith because He will cause us to arrive there together.

Another thing I would imagine many are pondering is, "I don't see how Achan relates to us in the Church today. After all, brother, that was the Old Covenant. We're under the New Covenant. I just don't see how this story of Joshua and Jericho applies to the Church now."

> **There should be no division in the body, but that the members should have the same care for one another.**
>
> **And if one member suffers, all the members suffer with it; if one member is honored, all the members rejoice with it .**
>
> **1 Corinthians 12:25-26 NASB**

Does any of this sound familiar? You see, according to my Bible, there are some constants that never change. One of those is God. He said, **For I am the Lord, I change not** (Malachi 3:6), and **Jesus Christ the same yesterday, and to day, and for ever** (Hebrews 13:8). Remember, God is a family God and He is committed to seeing that we learn to live, function and care for each other as a family unit — a corporate body. It can no longer be "every man for himself," but rather we must all become our brother's keeper whether we like it or not.

"Well, what does that mean?" That means that we must never allow ourselves to compromise what God is speaking to our local churches by hiding behind lame excuses such as, "But God, I didn't do it. He did it." No, that's not how it works. The scriptures teach that if one is hurt, then the whole body is hurt. If one is happy, then everyone should be happy. "But, that's not fair," you say. Quit thinking "Western civilization" and start thinking "like God!" You don't live your life for yourself, but rather "preferring one another in love" — we grow up in Him until we become like Him. It is His kingdom we are establishing and building, not our own, and without learning to walk together in unity we will never achieve what He desires for us to accomplish as His Church.

The devil is very aware of the power of unity. That's why he works overtime in trying to keep the body of Christ filled with leaven of all kinds. He knows that the scripture is true when it says, **A little leaven leavens the whole lump of dough** (Galatians 5:9, NASB). He also knows that whenever a people become united, the power of unity is released so as to guarantee their success. Remember the story of the tower of Babel? Even though the tower was being built for the glory of man rather than God, God Himself said,

> **Behold, the people is one, and they have all one language; and this they begin to do: and now nothing**

will be restrained from them, which they have imagined to do.

Genesis 11:6

In other words, God said, "These people can do anything and nothing will be impossible for them because they are working together in one accord." That's the power of unity and that's what is missing from most of our local churches today. We do not strive to walk in one accord but rather we allow "a little leaven" to destroy the entire work.

"Leaven. What on earth is leaven?" someone might be thinking. Leaven is a symbol of sin throughout the Bible. In our story about Joshua, Achan was the leaven that leavened the entire camp. Amazing, isn't it? One man's sin affected three million people. Why? Because it only takes a little leaven to mess up everything and everyone. That is why it is so important for us to be closely related, constantly exhorting, encouraging and challenging one another in the faith.

When God relates to His Church, His bride, then He deals with her corporately as one, not individually by member. He isn't willing simply to love her left foot, her elbows and the back of her head because they are loyal to Him. He wants the whole bride from head to toe. If the whole body can't make and honor the marriage covenant, then the marriage can't take place. Likewise, if the entire local church can't meet the requirements for a covenant promise, then even those individuals who did meet those requirements must suffer the loss of the blessing because of their fellow members who ignored God's Word. Leaven, sin, messes up everyone and everything it touches. That's why the Bible in the New Testament warns us of five specific types of leaven to watch for and avoid. Any one of these can enter a church and rob it of its unity and blessings almost overnight.

What are these five types of leaven? Well, Jesus told us to beware of the leaven of Herod, the leaven of the

Sadducees, and the leaven of the Pharisees. Paul told us to be aware of the leaven of the Corinthian church and of the Galatian church. Let's take a closer look at each one and see how they affect us today.

The "leaven of Herod" is the spirit of the world or worldliness. The Bible warns us, **And be not conformed to this world...** (Romans 12:2). There is a whole philosophy out there that is totally and diametrically opposed to how God thinks. Christians who fall into this perverted thinking blend into the sinful scenery perfectly — until the piercing eyes of God see through all the deception and strip away the excuses. This philosophy breeds and justifies things like fornication and adultery, abortion, "alternate lifestyles" (homosexuality), and quick divorce (if it doesn't work, fix it quick with a divorce). Rather than changing our thinking and being transformed into His likeness, this leaven contaminates the people and has them conform their "theology" to line up with their own perverted "morality." God will never allow this attitude to prevail. He will have a people "holy unto the Lord," and only in purging our churches of this leaven will we see God's blessing and favor in our midst.

The "leaven of the Sadducees" has to do with denying the power of God. This Jewish sect did not believe in the supernatural. Unfortunately, many people in the Church of Jesus today have allowed the leaven of the Sadducees to taint their lives. They don't believe in any supernatural manifestations. They don't believe in the resurrection, or signs and wonders, healing, or God's gifts to the Church, like apostles and prophets. The leaven of the Sadducees is crippling the Church in a big way today.

Then there's the "leaven of the Pharisees" which is the leaven of hypocrisy. It means "to pretend, to act" and it perfectly describes people who are self-righteous and judgmental. A hypocrite will look at a sinner who is seeking God and pray, "Thank You, God, that I'm not like that! I fast and pray, I tithe, and I do great humanitarian things for You." The truth is that "there is none righteous; no not one." None of us has the right to look down at another person just because they are struggling with sin in their life. We were once just as dirty and sinful as they are and "but for the grace of God, there go I."

The "leaven of the Corinthians" is the leaven of sensuality, carnality, and religious pride. People infected and tainted by this leaven will proudly tell you, "Well, brother, we have the gifts in our church. Yes sir, we operate in all the gifts — all nine. In fact, we operate in all in every service! Not only that, but we only have the biggest of the big boys come to our place and preach. We are the greatest!" Amazingly this was all true for the Corinthian church. They did have all that, but they also had incest, fornication, disorder at the Lord's table, rampant lawsuits between members of the church, drunkenness, division-breeding debates regarding the resurrection, and they maligned the preachers after every service. You talk about messed up, these folks were nowhere near what God intended for them, but rather than face it they hid behind the "leaven" until God forced them to handle it through the Apostle Paul's ministry.

I believe that of all the leavens we are warned about, this one is more prevalent in the American church than any of the others. When are we going to realize that it doesn't matter how much "power" we seem to have nor the amount of social influence we exert, the issue is, "Ye shall know them by their fruit," and many of our "finest" churches today have a lot of "rotten apples" in their pews.

Finally, there's the "leaven of the Galatians" — the spiritual carcinogen of legalism. This leaven is what divides us into various factions within the Church and produces sectarianism in the ranks. We insist on "mixing" God's

Word with some of our own works so we can "improve it" and "make it clearer." Those who allow this leaven to remain will work so hard at "clarifying" the Word that they find they can't really believe we were saved by faith and by grace. Their thinking becomes filled with the notion that, "Surely our works, (and boy, do we have some good ones) count for something. Grace alone is not enough. It's faith and works. Yes, I believe in Christ as my Lord and Savior, but I'm also going to keep the law of Moses, because it takes both to get you in." Ironic, isn't it? This logic, while totally unbiblical, cannot only lock a church into legalistic bondage for every member, it will also be the very thing they use to keep others out!

Leaven is a lot like cancer — it always starts small in an inconspicuous place, but it spreads at an almost uncontrollable rate if it isn't caught early. I assure you that God is committed to revealing the leaven if we are committed to dealing with it when it is revealed. Don't forget, our God is a family God, and He has carefully placed each of us in church families so as to fulfill our destiny in Him. Anything that destroys His family, God hates with a passion, and therefore He is not willing to allow anything or anyone to remain in His family who will harm it. That's why He had Paul to command the church at Corinth to expel its member involved in an incestuous relationship. God told them through the apostle, THROW HIM OUT! I know that seems pretty harsh, but God doesn't play with leaven. He deals with it swiftly. We should note, however, that in Paul's second letter to the Corinthians, he instructed them to restore the brother due to his repentance. God is indeed a God of love, but He is also a God of righteousness.

So, how do we recognize leaven, you might be wondering? Most of the time, evidence of leaven will show up in two basic areas: doctrinal offenses and behavioral offenses. When revealed, we must deal with these trespasses or sins if we want to keep the unity which gives the blessing. Never forget, the goal of the enemy in sowing leaven into our midst is to destroy the unity within the local body. He knows full well that "a house divided against itself will fall." That's why in the early church you find the Apostle Paul rebuking Alexander the coppersmith along with Hymenaeus and Philetus because their doctrine concerning the resurrection had crossed the line from personal opinion to heresy that directly contradicted the Scriptures, and the doctrine was beginning to subvert the faith of some of the sheep. (See 1 Timothy 1:19-20; 2 Timothy 2:17, 4:14.)

The apostle also had to administer some extreme correction in the areas of doctrine that is not according to godliness (1 Timothy 6:3-5), and the doctrine of idolatry and immorality. (Revelation 2:12-17.) He also addressed doctrine that brought division, that was contrary to the apostles' doctrine or teaching in Romans 16:17-18. Then there were the doctrines of devils and heresy. All of that to say this, in the eyes of God the Father, leaven is a very serious matter. That's why we are admonished in Scripture to immediately deal with the problems and problem-makers just as soon as they are discovered.

This brings us to a very serious problem within the American church. Most Christians within our churches do not understand the difference between forgiveness and discipline. These are two completely separate issues. We must always forgive a person if they're in sin just as God forgives the vilest of sinners the moment they call upon Him in repentance. Forgiveness, extended from one member of the body to another, is absolutely imperative, for the Word declares that if we retain their sin, then God retains ours! Just because one is forgiven, however, does not necessarily exempt them from discipline. Often, it is the discipline administered in love after forgiveness is granted that teaches us the lesson needed to not yield to the devil's trap again. That's why the Bible teaches us in Hebrews:

111

"My son, do not regard lightly the discipline of the Lord, nor faint when you are reproved by Him;

"For those whom the Lord loves He disciplines, and He scourges every son whom He receives."

All discipline for the moment seems not to be joyful, but sorrowful; yet to those who have been trained by it, afterwards it yields the peaceful fruit of righteousness.

Hebrews 12:5-6, 11 NASB

The aforementioned scripture is the key to understanding why we in leadership within the local church must be willing to administer biblical correction. Our people's lives are at stake, as is the blessing upon the corporate body which comes only from unity. God is not willing to just "slip-slide along" and let "whatever will be will be." He demands that we deal with the leaven when it is revealed and in love administer biblical discipline so that the individuals involved may learn from their mistakes and become more like Christ. Correction is never for the purpose of rejection, but rather restoration so that the unity of the body may be preserved.

As a senior pastor, I have experienced first-hand the growth and effectiveness unity enables a church to have. In our church, Evangel Church, unity has dramatically affected two key areas: Leadership decisions and staff organization. Allow me to explain.

Church government at Evangel is simple. We administer by the Acts 15 standard:

It seemed good unto us, being assembled with one accord, to send chosen men unto you with our beloved Barnabas and Paul.

For it seemed good to the Holy Ghost, and to us, to lay upon you no greater burden than these necessary things.

Acts 15:25,28

There you have it. It **seemed good to the Holy Ghost, and to us.** That's how we function in every major decision our eldership makes.

When I bring a matter before the church elders, we pray, discuss, confront, and work out every detail until we have a witness — until there is 100 percent agreement. In those rare times when we don't come into total agreement on a matter, then I step in as the chief or senior shepherd of the local church, and because of our understanding of God's government, the elders submit to my authority in the matter, still in one accord.

No, I'm not a dictator nor is my eldership made up of a bunch of "yes men." We simply believe that God knew what He was doing when He instituted His methods of government. If I or any other senior shepherd decides to stray out of agreement with God, then God is the safety leveler. He will always act to protect His flock and because the church leadership has maintained unanimity, He is able to proceed and remove any leader from their midst should they become a weak link in His purposes because of their sin or rebellion.

Our understanding of the power of unity has also dramatically affected the size and function of our local church staff. At one time, we had a paid staff of 75 people — along with a great deal of confusion. God began to deal with us about Gideon, who had a job to do and too many people tagging along for the ride. God showed His leader how to trim an army from 30,000 to 300. Why would God want to do this? Because the 29,700 were all united for the wrong purpose. They were united in their belief that they were going to fail. Their fear of failure was going to ensure Gideon's defeat. Once Gideon reduced his army, however, to the 300 "nuts" that dared to believe for the impossible, then the power of unity took over and a great victory was achieved for the glory of God.

In our situation, God led us to reduce our staff to 25 people who had the vision burned in their hearts for our local church, and who were joined to me and our leadership. We have been amazed to discover that these people accomplished more than what the 75 ever could do! God commanded the blessing upon us because of unity in the leadership and support staff of our local assembly.

I wonder what would happen if we amplified this tremendous truth we have learned and applied it to your local church. I think we might discover some real surprises even regarding some of the most familiar verses of scripture we feel we've mastered.

For instance, I don't know about you, but I have never experienced the situation described in Malachi 3:10 (though we quote it all the time as if we have):

> **...and prove me now herewith, saith the lord of hosts, if I will not open you the windows of heaven, and pour you out a blessing, that there shall not be room enough to receive it.**

I always seem to have plenty of room left to receive more from God! That means either God is a liar or we are doing something wrong. I believe the answer to be obvious since "God is not a man that He should lie."

The problem is that those verses are not addressed to individuals singularly. In Malachi 3:8-9, God made it clear that the whole nation had stolen from Him, although it is inconceivable to think that every person in Israel had failed to tithe and give offerings. Remember the incident with Achan. In the mind and perspective of God, if one person in a family, tribe or nation sins, all have sinned. Every time God's people came into total and complete unity in the Old and New Testaments, God always released a degree of corporate blessing that was far beyond any blessing that we've ever touched or known in the church today. So, if we desire to experience the "corporate blessing" promised in

Malachi, we must be willing to pay the price for unity in our corporate bodies.

Think about Ananias and Sapphira. Why did God kill them? All they did was lie. Why, if next Sunday morning God decided to kill everyone in your church who had lied, how many would be left standing after the smoke had cleared? What made this case so unusual?

God faced a unique dilemma in Acts chapter 5. More than 50,000 saints belonged to the first church in human history, and some scholars believe there were as many as 70,000. Evidently, there were two souls who were out of unity, Ananias and Sapphira. I believe God thought, "I will have to withhold the corporate blessing from My family unless I take these sinners out of the picture. No, I will not allow the entire church to suffer for these two mistakes — I will let My people experience what I want the Church to experience — the power of being in one accord, holding all things in common." That decision being made, God removed the offending members and thereby the first church experienced tremendous growth and blessing.

So, what about now? Does God, Himself, remove the offending members from our midst, or do we do it ourselves? Good question. Let's see if we can answer it.

As far as I can discern from Scripture, there are three groups qualified to administer correction and discipline regarding leaven within the Church. The first, of course, is God Himself. This would be as in the aforementioned illustration where God sovereignly administers the discipline. The second group would be those who are recognized as the spiritual leadership members of the body as described in Galatians 6:1. And finally, the entire Church and every member of it can be involved in this process as outlined in Matthew 18:15-18. The bottom line, however, is this—no matter which group is utilized in getting the leaven out, it must be gotten out! To allow it to remain will rob us of all that He has destined our churches to do.

Remember: Wherever there is total unity in the church, there will also be unusual levels of blessing, anointing, and power. You can't stop it! God, Himself, will see to it that your church becomes one of the greatest churches in your area simply because you are walking together "in one accord." God, help us all to attain to this standard.

6

Prayer and Corporate Destiny

No study of God's destiny for the Church would be complete without thoroughly examining God's method of achieving His intended will for our corporate lives, that is, implementing the finished work of the head Jesus Christ on this earth. Just how are we to accomplish this great commission He left us: **Go ye therefore, and teach all nations...** (Matthew 28:19)? Consider the following:

> **For though we walk in the flesh, we do not war according to the flesh,**
> **For the weapons of our warfare are not of the flesh, but divinely powerful for the destruction of fortresses.**
> **We are destroying speculations and every lofty thing raised up against the knowledge of God, and we are taking every thought captive to the obedience of Christ,**
> **And we are ready to punish all disobedience, whenever your obedience is complete.**
>
> **2 Corinthians 10:3-6 NASB**

You see, there is a plan to accomplish His will, but I have discovered that the church knows so very little about how God truly taught us to pray, we spend most of our time "asking for stuff" rather than waging warfare that destroys strongholds and secures victory. Maybe it would help to digress just for a moment and remind us of things we are supposed to already know.

Before God ever created the world, He had already decided to rule this planet through His unique creation—man — destined from the beginning to have dominion over the earth. God said, **Let Us make man in Our image,**

117

according to Our likeness; and let them rule... (Genesis 1:26 NASB). The "first Adam" failed and came short of God's purposes for his life, causing both spiritual and physical death to come into our lives, but God also had a plan to redeem His creation.

This was accomplished by sending the "last Adam" — a perfect man "born" but not "created" — God's only begotten Son. Through His death, burial, resurrection and ascension, Jesus Christ has translated us out of darkness. Now, we are in Christ, and together we make up the body of this last Adam, this ruler of the earth, and it is only in coming into a complete understanding of who we are in Christ that we will be able to effectively accomplish all He has left for us to do.

So, that brings us back to the question, "How do we do it?" If prayer is the key, then "how do we pray?" More than that, "How do we know how to pray?" Who teaches us what to do?

> **And my message and my preaching were not in persuasive words of wisdom, but in demonstration of the Spirit and of power,**
>
> **That your faith should not rest on the wisdom of man but on the power of God.**
>
> **But we speak God's wisdom in a mystery, the hidden wisdom, which God predestined before the ages to our glory;**
>
> **For to us God revealed them through the Spirit; for the Spirit searches all things, even the depths of God.**
>
> **Now we have received, not the spirit of the world, but the Spirit who is from God, that we might know the things freely given to us by God,**
>
> **Which things we also speak, not in words taught by human wisdom, but in those taught by the Spirit, combining spiritual thoughts with spiritual words.**
>
> **But a natural man does not accept the things of the Spirit of God.**
>
> **But we have the mind of Christ.**
>
> **1 Corinthians 2:4-5,7,10,12-14,16 NASB**

There it is. There's our answer. The Spirit, Himself, will instruct us regarding the mind of Christ as we submit ourselves to the Lord in prayer. It is during our prayer time with the Father that the guidance and wisdom we need will be transferred from His infinite intelligence and Spirit to our finite understanding housed in this "temple of flesh." As we spend time with Him in prayer we will discover many tools, helps and abilities that He has provided to assist us in establishing His kingdom on this earth. Regardless, however, of all the "helps" we may discover, the bottom line is this: Prayer is the only method we have to implement the finished work of the Lord Jesus Christ, for it is only through prayer that we will have the knowledge of how to put the tools, helps and abilities together in such a way as to accomplish His intended results.

You may be thinking, "Man, this is going to be hard work! I mean, how am I ever going to learn enough to do everything God wants done?" Have I got good news for you. There's nothing for us to "do" except obey whatever He tells us. You see, Jesus, Himself, has already "done" everything necessary for you and me to accomplish His will for our lives and the lives of those He charges us with. That's right. He's done everything, and we don't have to "add" anything to what Jesus has already done. He has provided everything necessary to redeem our race, and all we need do is obey Him in the simple tasks He entrusts us with which allows His finished work to manifest itself in lives that are in need.

That brings us to a major point which I want to address in this chapter. Until now, I have taught you about your personal destiny, the church's destiny, the importance of joining and the absolute necessity of local churches being united as one. You might be thinking that all I'm trying to do is teach you how to be powerful and successful, with no thought or regard to the lost and dying who are unreached in our world. Nothing could be farther from the truth, but until you understand the aforementioned topics, you are not ready for the revelation which I'm going to give you in this chapter regarding harvesting souls for Christ. You see, while I believe that some tasks can be accomplished by individual believers for the Lord, I further believe the greatest tasks can only be accomplished by a church united in one heart, one mind and one accord through prayer. Every time the miraculous has exploded on an entire nation, it has been those rare times when God's people laid aside their differences and came together in prayer and unity. Yes, I believe the greatest harvest of souls the world has ever seen is yet to be brought in, but I do not believe any one individual is going to accomplish this task. I believe it is going to happen as local churches in one accord begin to pray properly as God taught us in the Bible to pray for His harvest.

Now, that brings up an interesting question. Just what does the Bible teach about how the Church is to pray for the lost? I think before we attempt to answer that, however, we better answer the question of what is the key to effective prayer in our individual lives as well as the Church corporately.

The Bible teaches that we are many individual members, yet we are one in Christ. He is the Vine, and we are the branches, is the way John puts it. (John 15:5.) When we first enter His kingdom, we often try to align God with our needs and prayer requests. As we grow more mature and allow our relationship with our Creator to deepen in intimacy, we learn to do and pray for things according to His will, by His name — not according to our will or purposes. We begin to pray according to His character, according to His Word, and according to His Spirit. By yielding to this learned process, we continue to put off the nature of the old man as we replace him with the nature of our new man in Christ Jesus. (See Ephesians 4:22, Colossians 3:8-9.)

The path of success in our Christian walk is a daily process of laying down our life to be conformed to the image of Christ. For our personalities to manifest the godly qualities of His personality and for us to accomplish His purposes, a lifelong weeding-out process is required. True prayer is the process of learning His lordship. Not our will, but His will. Not our way, but His way. Not our life, but His life. That's what the world needs to see, Christ in us, the hope of glory. We must manifest Christ to the world.

Obviously, the only way we can accomplish this is by bearing fruit in our lives that reveals Christ to those we meet. The scriptures declare, **Taste and see that the Lord is good...** (Psalm 34:8). There are countless numbers of hungry people in our generation, and it is our responsibility to bear godly fruit so that the hungry can be fed from our abundance. Our objective is to lead a life of prayer and obedience that allows the life of Christ in us to be released as Spirit-empowered fruit. We are the branches, and our responsibility as fruit-bearers is to ask God for the harvest of Christ-like fruit that will attract and heal the heathen. **And I, if I be lifted up from the earth, will draw all men unto me** (John 12:32). Wherever the Christ in us is lifted up, we will see the wounded, the bound, the hungry and the desperate coming to us to partake of the "fruit" which is "healing to the nations." (See Revelation 22:2.)

Okay — so far we've established the fact that we are to rule and transform the world around us by revealing the dominion of the Christ in us that is subject to divine order. We've also established that prayer is the most important element in fulfilling this task. So, now we need to address the most important question of all, and that is, "How do we pray?" What do we say and how do we ask for whatever it is we're supposed to be praying for or about? (If this sounds confusing, then congratulate yourself. The majority of the body of Christ is confused when it comes to prayer and the implementation of it.)

The Bible does not really give us any set prayers or formulas under the New Testament, because the Bible is not a prayer book. The three most important words in the Bible that have to do with prayer are: intercession, supplication and petition. All of these obviously have to do with "asking" for something, but what is it that we are supposed to ask for? How do we learn to pray?

The New Testament is composed primarily of letters that the early Christian leaders wrote to one another. They had no idea that the entire body of Christ would ultimately read those letters and therefore they addressed specific situations that were needing attention within the local church at that time. It's interesting to note that little has changed over the past 2,000 years with regard to Church problems and needs. The writings of these early apostles and leaders are as current today as they were the day they were written.

As we read these letters, we can almost hear them talking one to another and we can even "overhear" them praying. AHA! The best way to learn anything in God is by example. Maybe all we need do is listen to what they said about prayer and fulfilling God's will — particularly the Apostle Paul. He was a tremendous man of prayer, and as a result of the fruitfulness of his life, he was privileged to write the majority of the New Testament.

Before embarking upon this journey into the life of the Apostle Paul, let me ask you a question. Have you ever wondered how or why Saul, who became Paul, was initially converted? I mean, he really wasn't the kind of fellow most of us would court if we were looking for a "ministerial candidate." Saul was one mean dude — and he hated the Christian church with a passion. In fact, when he was confronted by the presence of God, he was traveling to Damascus on another mission to persecute Christians under the authority and full approval of the Jewish Sanhedrin. You see, Saul had already won a reputation for his zeal. He had arrested, imprisoned and evidently killed many Christian Jews in the name of God. He was a powerful man with major political and religious clout and unbelievable determination. He certainly wasn't seeking Jesus for himself. He hated this new doctrine, which he believed to be of the devil, and yet in spite of this strong opposition to the truth, God apprehended him for His service. Why and how did He do that?

I believe that God met Saul on that Damascus road because some group of Christians was praying, "My God, deliver us from this madman who is coming to put us in prison! Help us, Jesus, and please hurry!" In fact, in my own heart and spirit, I believe that Ananias carried the heaviest burden of prayer for the saints in Damascus. I can almost hear him praying, "God, You know about this man called Saul, and You have to do something, God. I ask You to deliver us from that heathen, in the name of Jesus, Your Son."

Through their prayers, those fearful Christians in Damascus released a power that totally blinded Saul on the way to their city and confronted him with the presence of the living God who asked, "Why are you persecuting Me?" You talk about having someone's undivided attention! Saul must have thought, "No, it can't be! I persecute people who follow You!" To God, however, when you touch His people, you have touched Him personally. I find it very interesting that God revealed Himself to Saul, but did not reveal either the direction or the purpose for his life. He just blinded him and put him in a motel room. (See Acts 9:1-9.)

You know why He did that? Because when we pray for something or someone, we become responsible for being utilized in the fulfillment of whatever we are praying. Now the Lord appears to Ananias and says, "I want you to go to Saul of Tarsus — he is your responsibility. He is waiting and praying in a motel room."

Can't you just imagine how amazed Ananias must have been? I think the younger generation probably would have said "freaked out!" "Who, me, God? You've gotta be kidding! I asked You to do something with him...but, I didn't expect You to deliver him into my hands. How do I know his conversion is real?" Now, as if God telling Ananias to go minister to Saul wasn't enough, He also told him, "Ananias, this man is My chosen instrument to take My name before the Gentiles, kings and the sons of Israel. Now, go take care of him." I can hear him mumbling all the way there. (See Acts 9:10-16.)

By the time Ananias met Saul, that Jewish zealot had not eaten or drunk anything for three days. He was totally blind, but he was a changed man. Still reeling from his experience on the Damascus road, he had many questions; but he also had some answers for the first time in his life. Having been in constant prayer for the three days since his divine encounter, he awaited the arrival of someone who would tell him what to do next and begin the instruction process that would release him to fulfill the call of God on his life.

Saul had always "known" that Jehovah was real. He had done all that the law prescribed, and he was a recognized rabbi and scholar of Hebrew law, but now he had encountered Jesus in a heavenly vision, and had been smitten blind for three days. The great Saul of Tarsus had made Jesus his own Messiah and Lord, and he was just waiting for orders. Now it was time to act, but only according to God's plan. Prayer helps us to realize God's way to do something. Sometimes we can only possess the things of God through submitted prayer.

Can't you see Ananias coming to introduce himself to the one man everybody in the Damascus church feared? They had heard about this man from refugee Christian Jews who had passed through Damascus in their flight from Jerusalem carrying what worldly goods they could salvage before Saul and his men had raided their meetings. They had heard about the arrests, the trials, the terrible imprisonments, and they had heard that Saul had held the clothing of the elders in his support of the stoning of young Stephen....

And now, here he was! Somebody's prayers had worked, and no one was ready for what happened after that! Can't you just see Ananias taking Paul to one of the church services in Damascus? As everyone looked up, they saw the familiar face of Ananias, but there was someone in his shadow that they didn't recognize. Even those in the back could see the familiar clothing of a Pharisee from the temple congregation in Jerusalem, the expensive cloth and flawless seams...GASP! It was Saul, the agent sent by the Sanhedrin to seize every Christian he found!

I can imagine the hush that swept through the congregation, followed by loud murmurs and shouts as a number of men quickly moved across the aisle to take the hands of their wives and usher them toward the door, only to hear Ananias shout, "Wait! Stop, my brothers! We have been praying about this man — our Lord has met him on the Damascus road, and Saul has seen the light of the Messiah, Jesus Christ!"

To say that they welcomed him with "open arms" would be a bit much. I'm sure many questioned whether or not he was sincerely converted or just pretending to be so that he could infiltrate their ranks and plan to entrap them. Ironically, God used those Jewish Christians at Damascus to teach and to train the man who would one day evangelize the whole Gentile world and write most of the New Testament epistles. Talk about "prayer changing things"!

And that brings us back to the purpose of this digression on the conversion of Paul. Any study of his life reveals that whenever he moved into a new stage in his spiritual life, it was always in the context of prayer. Why? Because Paul learned early in his walk with the Lord that the only plans that ultimately succeeded were the ones birthed in and through prayer. It was only after sixteen or seventeen years of intense training, that the Spirit of God said (after several men of God had ministered to the Lord in prayer and fasting), **Set apart for Me Barnabas and Saul for the work**

to which I have called them (Acts 13:2 NASB). Out of prayer, Saul was sent forth with Barnabas to evangelize. He had no advertising plan, no crusade ministry, no auditorium — he didn't even have a P.A. system!

What he did have was a sure word from God that came out of prayer. Because it was a sure word, he successfully faced both the Jews and the Gentiles, neither of which were especially happy to receive him because he didn't preach what they wanted to hear.

The Jews were looking for a Messiah Who would deliver them from the Romans, and Paul preached that the Messiah had already come and that He had set up a spiritual kingdom on earth. The Jews didn't want to hear that — they wanted a soldier/king as the Messiah Who would restore the throne of David and get rid of the Romans.

The Gentiles, on the other hand, were required to worship the Roman emperor as a god. They were told that Caesar was lord of lords, and that he was the god of every citizen of Rome. Whenever a nation was conquered for Rome, they had the responsibility to offer incense on a flaming altar and recognize that Caesar was king and the god of all gods. They were told that Caesar was the lord of the universe, so the last thing they wanted to hear was about the true Lord of lords named Jesus Christ Who ruled the universe.

Paul knew that his preaching of the gospel would not occur in a friendly, laid-back atmosphere. So, how did he establish churches and strengthen their faith in such adverse conditions? Paul wrote that the weapons he used were not of the flesh. (2 Corinthians. 10:4.) He fulfilled his mission using divine weapons, and He refused to use emotional gimmicks to persuade people. He taught Christians to fight against the spiritual forces that came against their fulfillment of divine destiny. He waged war with spiritual weapons which were so strong they could pull down the fortresses in the minds of men and change their way of thinking. They could bring into captivity every thought that was outside of the mind of the Lord, and the underlying motivation of these weapons was prayer.

In fact, as we study Paul's epistles, prayer seems to be the main weapon he used to help believers grow. So, I guess we better answer the question, how did Paul pray for the churches he established? Consider the following: **Night and day praying exceedingly that we might see your face, and might perfect that which is lacking in your faith?** (1 Thessalonians 3:10). To the church at Colossae, he wrote, **We have not ceased to pray for you...** (Colossians 1:9 NASB). To the church at Philippi, he wrote, **I thank my God in all my remembrance of you, always offering prayer with joy in my every prayer for you all.** (Philippians 1:3-4 NASB). In Romans 1:9 (NASB), Paul wrote, **...unceasingly I make mention of you.** And to the Ephesians he said, **For this reason I too...do not cease giving thanks for you, while making mention of you in my prayers** (Ephesians 1:15,16 NASB).

In writing to Timothy in 2 Timothy 1:3 (NASB), Paul said, **I constantly remember you in my prayers night and day.** Now, I want you to notice the words Paul uses in the few passages we've examined. He talks about praying day and night, unceasingly, earnestly, constantly, and always in remembrance of these young Christians. Paul's life and patterns of prayer tell us that he thought there was something so important about prayer that he had to do it day and night on behalf of the churches he had planted.

I believe the reason Paul invested his time and emphasis in prayer was because he understood this was the only way to bring about the finished work of Christ upon this earth. Furthermore, Paul not only assumed the responsibility of praying for these churches he established, but as a true mentor, he laid the same responsibility on them! In 1 Thessalonians 5:17, he urged the believers there to pray without ceasing. In the book of Ephesians, Paul told the saints,

> **With all prayer and petition pray at all times in the Spirit, and with this in view, be on the alert with all perseverance and petition for all the saints,**
> **And pray on my behalf....**
>
> Ephesians 6:18-19 NASB

Paul was saying here, "Look, I never stop praying for you. Night and day I am unceasingly mentioning you in my prayers to the Lord. Now I am asking you to pick up that responsibility. I want you to begin to pray night and day for saints everywhere, and especially for me."

In the Book of Colossians, believers are told, **Devote yourselves to prayer, keeping alert in it with an attitude of thanksgiving; praying at the same time for us as well, that God may open up to us a door for the word...** (Colossians 4:2-3 NASB). The Greek word for "devote" here actually means "don't take a vacation." Think about that! No vacation — this is it for the rest of your life. You are to become addicted to this. Prayer must become your foremost reason for living.

If you're a pastor as I am, the question may be coming to you, "If this guy really spent that much time in prayer, when did he have time to plan his strategy in taking the gospel to the Jews and Gentiles?" The answer I have come to is, he didn't! Paul didn't have any confidence in his own flesh or natural ability. First of all, earthly warfare with natural weapons and abilities was useless against spiritual forces. Besides that, many times he didn't speak very well. He often came to places in fear and trembling, saying "I need wisdom from God." So he prayed, and the wisdom came not with enticing words of men, but in demonstration of the Spirit's power. (1 Corinthians 2:4.) It was no accident that everyone Paul came into contact with became involved in that same attitude of prayer.

By now, I can imagine many of you are saying to yourselves, "That's what I want too. I want to be a man or woman of prayer and get the results Paul got." I believe that to be a godly desire, but for that to happen in your life we must now address the question of just exactly how did Paul pray? I think you're going to be surprised at what we find.

If I were to ask you what your number one prayer responsibility was, what would your answer be? I can tell you what most folks would say. They would say their number one prayer responsibility was to pray for the lost to be saved, and I must confess that answer certainly sounds correct in light of John 3:16,

> **For God so loved the world, that he gave his only begotten Son, that whosoever believeth in him should not perish, but have everlasting life.**

God does indeed love sinners and wills that none should perish, but just where do we get the idea that we are to spend all our time praying for the lost? To be sure, the Bible instructs us to show love to the lost, share with the lost, have compassion on the lost, minister to the lost and even go the extra mile for the lost — but, where does it tell us to spend all our time in prayer for the lost? "Well, if we don't pray for the lost, who do we pray for?" you ask. Now that's really a good question. Let's look more closely at it and see if we can find an answer out of Paul's life.

In the Apostle Paul's life you will discover this very extraordinary thing about his time in prayer, he rarely ever prayed for the lost. What he did "night and day" was pray for the church that she might reach the lost with the gospel message. In fact, whenever Paul learned of someone turning from sin and beginning to live for Jesus, he always made them a regular part of his daily prayers.

> **For this reason I too, having heard of the faith in the Lord Jesus which exists among you, and your love for all the saints,**
>
> **Do not cease giving thanks for you, while making mention of you in my prayers.**
>
> **Ephesians 1:15-16 NASB**

This is really quite a revelation. When Paul learned that some people in Ephesus had professed faith in Christ, and had begun to display love towards other saints, that did something for him; and he immediately added them to his continual prayer life. In fact, it would appear that Paul was basically saying, "Before I could pray this way for you and invest my prayer time in you, I had to hear about two things: First, your faith in God, and secondly, your love toward other believers."

Paul reiterates this to the church in Colossae when he writes, praying always for you, since we heard of your faith in Christ Jesus and the love you have for all saints (Colossians 1:3-4.)

"So, what are you trying to say," you ask? Simply this. According to the teachings of Paul, the only people who got a lot of his time in prayer were believers — not sinners. Why? Because rather than spend his time praying for people who didn't even know they had a need, Paul spent his time praying for the believers in the church that they might take the gospel to the lost and not only reveal their great need, but meet it through salvation in Jesus Christ.

Many of us don't understand how important this pattern or principle is. We need to ingrain this pattern of prayer into our thinking because it makes a difference in how we pray for people. No longer should we spend our time praying for God to bless the lost, but rather we should pray for the saints that they will be faithful to the One Who called them and share Christ with all they meet.

Having said that, I need to point out that most Christians really do not understand what they have already received in Christ — that's why most of our praying is for ourselves to get things. It usually goes something like this: "God, do something for me. God, do something in this situation — Give me some more of You. I need something more. Give me deliverance." And on and on it goes. The problem with these sincere prayers is that they contradict what the Bible teaches. According to the Word of God, He has already granted these prayers through the birth, death, resurrection and ascension of the Lord Jesus Christ. His work of redemption is a finished work. There is nothing we can add to it and there is nothing more He needs to do to it. It is a complete, finished work in and of itself.

Most of the time, all we do in our prayers is say, "Gimme, gimme, gimme" in different ways. Every time, God says, "I have given you everything that pertains to life and godliness. (See 2 Peter 1:3.) I gave My life; it is finished. I have done everything I was supposed to do." But, wait a minute, you say. I thought prayer involved intercession, supplication and petition — three forms of asking.

You're right. I guess our problem must be that we are "asking amiss" (James 4:3). Huh? The key to understanding what I'm trying to teach you here is in realizing what we have already received in Christ. That's what Paul prayed. He prayed that the believers within the local churches would come into a full understanding as to who they were and what they possessed in Christ.

> **Wherefore I also, after I heard of your faith in the Lord Jesus, and love unto all the saints,**
>
> **Cease not to give thanks for you, making mention of you in my prayers;**
>
> **That the God of our Lord Jesus Christ, the Father of glory, may give unto you the spirit of wisdom and revelation in the knowledge of him.**
>
> **Ephesians 1:15-17**

Paul prayed that these new believers would receive a **spirit of wisdom and revelation in the knowledge of him.** Paul was not praying that these people would come to Jesus — they were already believers. The problem was that these young Christians were like little newborn babies: Their eyes weren't fully open yet. That's why Paul prayed that they would receive a spirit of wisdom and revelation.

> **The eyes of your understanding being enlightened;
> that ye may know what is the hope of his calling, and
> what the riches of the glory of his inheritance in the
> saints,**
>
> **And what is the exceeding greatness of his power to
> us-ward who believe, according to the working of his
> mighty power.**
>
> **Ephesians 1:18-19**

Paul prayed that the eyes of the hearts of these young
believers would be enlightened so they could know three
important things: first, they needed to understand the hope
of the Lord's calling (Christ in you, the hope of glory).
Secondly, the spiritual eyes of these believers needed to be
opened to see "the riches of the glory of His inheritance in
them, in the saints" (the gates of hell shall not prevail
against them — the church). Thirdly, these believers needed
to perceive "the surpassing greatness of His power toward
them since they had believed" (greater is He who is in us,
than he who is in the world). They needed to understand
that this power was "in accordance with the working of the
strength of His might" (by My Spirit, saith the Lord).

These powerful revelations, Paul knew, were essential if
the early Church was to totally fulfill the Father's destiny
for them corporately. That's why Paul prayed for their
"eyes to be opened." He knew they had a vision problem
and couldn't really see what God wanted them to see.
That's why he spent so much time in prayer for the saints
because until they could see and understand all that Jesus
had done for them, they would never "deliver the goods"
to a lost and needy world.

So, how does this realization impact our prayer life?
Again, looking at the life of Paul, he says we need spiritual
wisdom and understanding so we can walk in a manner
worthy of the Lord. (Colossians 1:10.)

> **For this cause we also, since the day we heard it,
> do not cease to pray for you, and to desire that ye might**

be filled with the knowledge of his [God's] will in all wisdom and spiritual understanding;

That ye might walk worthy of the Lord unto all pleasing, being fruitful in every good work, and increasing in the knowledge of God;

Strengthened with all might, according to his glorious power, unto all patience and longsuffering with joyfulness.

Colossians 1:9-11

We are all called to please God in every good work and increase in the knowledge of Him. This is not a "one-time experience." We grow in wisdom and knowledge constantly as we walk with the Lord, because the spirit of wisdom and revelation continually reveal who we are in Christ. According to the Apostle Paul, we are already strengthened with all the power we will ever need for the attaining of all steadfastness and patience.... (Colossians 1:11.) Paul continually labored in prayer because his spiritual children still did not understand who they were in Christ, or why they had been born again. He was determined to pray until they saw their calling as God wanted them to see it.

The same problem plagues the Church today, but until we begin to pray properly one for another, covering one another in love (and nothing is more loving than praying one for another), and standing together for the Father's purpose to be accomplished through our lives and churches, then we will not see the harvest of souls He desires nor His kingdom established as He commanded. It is time for us to understand that we are God's inheritance. We must begin to perceive the power that's already in us, and our prayers must begin to show it.

Now are you beginning to see what Paul is trying to say in one epistle after another? If you do, this truth will transform the way we pray for each other and our churches! Paul is saying that when he prays for believers in these churches, he doesn't see them as they are now; he sees them as they are in Jesus Christ. He sees what they are destined to be in Christ. In searching the entire New Testament, I have not found one time that Paul prayed any differently for the Church. His heart's desire was for them to come into the revelation knowledge of who they are in Christ.

As I have begun to pattern my prayer life after this teaching from Paul, I have discovered a very important truth. Revelation knowledge comes with faithfulness in your prayer life. How you pray for yourself and others in the church is extremely important. This understanding has changed my concept and the whole way I view people. Before I learned to pray by revelation, I used to look at a Christian with a "lukewarm" attitude and pray, "God, light a fire under them. Take them through the valley of the shadow, Lord. I'm so sick of these lukewarm people. Why do you permit them to continue in their immature ways?"

In reality, these believers are lukewarm because they have not allowed the spirit of wisdom and revelation to change their lives. Now I'm learning to pray that they would see their destiny in God. Do you see how our prayers for the unsaved have limited God's intervention? God doesn't need us telling Him what to do; nor does He need us begging Him for someone's life repeatedly. Salvation for the lost has been made available already. (God's instrument for reaching the lost is walking around our churches on two feet! All the parts are here, now.) What we need to do is pray for a spirit of wisdom and revelation to bring us to a place of ministering by His Spirit. The most important prayer that you and I can pray is that we and our brothers and sisters in Christ will finally see who we are in God through the Spirit of wisdom and revelation.

"Well, what about Jesus?" you ask. He prayed for the lost, didn't He? The only recorded prayer we have of Jesus, other than being in the Garden of Gethsemane, is found in

John 17, and He did not pray for the lost in that prayer — He prayed for His disciples and those who would follow them. (Now, before you get all bent out of shape and start hollering about "The Lord's Prayer," I must point out that this isn't a "prayer" at all but rather a principle in narrative teaching form to motivate the disciples to prayer. Betcha thought you had me that time, huh?)

What Jesus actually said in John 17 was,

> **I pray for them** [the disciples]: **I pray not for the world, but for them which thou hast given me; for they are thine.**
>
> **Verse 9**

Now, why would Jesus pray like that? Because He has chosen to reveal Himself to mankind through "vessels of clay" and we need to have our eyes enlightened so that we can see ourselves the way God sees us in Christ. That's why Paul devoted his prayer time for the people who would be talking to the unconverted, not for the unconverted themselves.

As we bring this chapter to a close, let me ask you a question. What do we devote our prayer time to? It has been my experience that most of our private and corporate prayers major on "the person at work who is an alcoholic, and their marriage is in trouble," or "there are people who live in my community and they are sinners in darkness — I want us to pray today that God will do something for them, that He will give something to these people who need salvation," and on and on it goes.

When we pray like that, we are praying as if the New Testament never happened! We have continually bombarded God with prayers asking Him to do what He has already done. Why? Because, we want to avoid doing what God has told us to do. You and I are Christ in the flesh. We have been given the responsibility of bringing the kingdom of God upon the earth. To reiterate, Jesus said:

All power is given unto me in heaven and in earth.
Go ye therefore, and teach all nations.
Matthew 28:18-19

He prepared the way, now it is up to us to lead them into a greater understanding of life. We are supposed to go and tell them it is done. We are supposed to say, "Your sins are forgiven." Jesus told us to go. We are supposed to let His healing power flow out of us. We are the supernatural people who reveal signs and wonders as we proclaim the Good News.

Prayer is not, "Give it to me, God." Rather, it's "Reveal Yourself to me, Lord." It's the cry of a believer's heart that says, "God, I want to know who I am — give me a spirit of revelation and wisdom that I may be used to bring the light into the darkness and thereby rescue those who are perishing. Use me, Jesus — use me."

Once you and I begin to pray like that, then praying for the Church to thrust forth the harvesters into the fields will become second nature to us. Our churches are filled with workers; the only problem is to get them out of the churches and into the fields. Their weapons of warfare are already supplied and in place. All we need is to be in our place, willing to work, and filled with the knowledge of the power God has already planted within us.

For a church to fulfill its corporate destiny in God, it must learn to pray God's way. Jesus prayed for His disciples and those who would come after them. The disciples prayed for every believer in every church they pioneered or heard about through a faithful testimony. We must pray for our leadership and the harvesters in the pews so that the whole earth may be filled with His glory and men and women will run into the brightness of His dawning. The harvest is simply waiting for God's people to walk into their destiny.

7

The Towel of Servanthood

The anger simmered just below the surface as they hid their eyes from him. The atmosphere was hostile as he looked at the slightly built Jewish mother and her two brawny boys. In three-and-a-half years of travel together in the band, his companions had fought and squabbled endlessly over this issue. Now it had boiled to the surface with more heat and anger than they dreamed. Most of them thought Peter would be the one to lance the boil of this resentment over who would be second in command. The men didn't know it, but they were about to learn the secret of leadership in the Great Kingdom.

> Then came to him the mother of Zebedee's children with her sons, worshipping him, and desiring a certain thing of him.
>
> And he said unto her, What wilt thou? She saith unto him, Grant that these my two sons may sit, the one on thy right hand, and the other on the left, in thy kingdom.
>
> But Jesus answered and said, Ye know not what ye ask. Are ye able to drink of the cup that I shall drink of, and to be baptized with the baptism that I am baptized with? They say unto him, We are able.
>
> And he saith unto them, Ye shall drink indeed of my cup, and be baptized with the baptism that I am baptized with: but to sit on my right hand, and on my left, is not mine to give, but it shall be given to them for whom it is prepared of my Father.
>
> And when the ten heard it, they were moved with indignation against the two brethren.

But Jesus called them unto him, and said, Ye know that the princes of the Gentiles exercise dominion over them, and they that are great exercise authority upon them.

But it shall not be so among you: but whosoever will be great among you, let him be your minister;

And whosoever will be chief among you, let him be your servant:

Even as the Son of man came not to be ministered unto, but to minister, and to give his life a ransom for many.

Matthew 20:20-28

When the mother of James and John walked up to Jesus, the other ten disciples were watching, and they were getting angrier with every word they overheard. *She wants to make her boys somebody,* they thought secretly. The four gospels make it clear that the twelve disciples really only fought over one major issue: Who was number two after Jesus?

When Jesus saw the sons of Zebedee approach with their mother, He knew exactly what she would ask and why, but He asked her anyway, "What do you wish?" That is such an important question. He wanted her to speak it out for several reasons. First, He would make good use of this opportunity to teach His rough disciples, and those of us who would follow centuries later, about God's school of leadership.

The second reason he asked her to speak was prophetic in nature. The wife of Zebedee said,

Command that in Your kingdom these two sons of mine may sit, one on Your right and one on Your left.
Matthew 20:21 NASB

This mother's insight was far above that of most of Christ's followers — even among the twelve. Why? She may have been selfish, but she perceived that Jesus was more than just a great teacher and prophet. In her shrewd insight, when she looked at this man raised in a carpenter's home, she saw a King, for only kings have kingdoms, and she asked Him, **Command that in Your kingdom....**

I admire this woman for her tremendous depth of perception; no one else around Jesus perceived it. Jesus didn't even preach this message, but nevertheless, this woman understood that He was the King — even though she demonstrated the same confused idea about kingdom functions and leadership principles as we do today! Jesus responded with words that we need to heed today, **Ye know not what ye ask...**

I love to go to prayer meetings at our church. I like to quietly kneel down and listen to other people pray. I've discovered most Christians who are frustrated in prayer and ministry either "have not because they ask not," or they "ask amiss" or improperly. This is especially true when it comes to "their ministry."

Most Christians ask for what they see others possess in God. They pray, "God, if I can just be a pastor like Brother Don Meares, that would satisfy me" or "God, if You can just give me a national ministry so I can change thousands of lives — You know, on television and stuff." Maybe you have asked God to help you be "a great teacher in the Body of Christ" or, "God, if You would just give me a singing ministry, I would be totally fulfilled and happy. Yes, that's what I want. Give me that, God, and I will be fulfilled." The fact is that if you knew what that ministry cost, if you knew the price that person you envy had to pay to get what they have in God, you probably wouldn't ask for their ministry!

Jesus asked a question that everyone called to the ministry must face sooner or later. He asked the two brothers, **...Are ye able to drink of the cup that I shall drink of, and to be baptized with the baptism that I am baptized with? They say unto Him, We are able** (Matthew

20:22). It is easy to assume something where there is ignorance. They said, "Come on, bring us the cup. No, we don't know what the cup is, but we can drink it! Why no, Jesus. We have no idea what You are talking about (we feel that way a lot of the time), but yes, we know we can drink the cup."

They didn't realize that the cup Jesus would drink was death, nor that their destiny would lead them to drink the same cup in His name. "Can you drink the cup?" This drama didn't take place in secret, and what happened next offers the key to leadership in the kingdom of God. "Can you drink the cup?"

> **And he saith unto them, Ye shall drink indeed of my cup, and be baptized with the baptism that I am baptized with: but to sit on my right hand, and on my left, is not mine to give, but it shall be given to them for whom it is prepared of my Father.**
>
> **And when the ten heard it, they were moved with indignation against the two brethren.**
>
> **Matthew 20:23-24**

The Bible says that after the ten heard Jesus' reply to the three, they became indignant with the two brothers. Now we have a realistic picture of life in the fast lanes at nearly every major church and ministry in this country! Who are the ten? They are the disciples of Jesus. We're talking about the disciples who would become foundations in the early Church. The mother of James and John had come to Jesus because she wanted to make her boys somebody, and the other ten men were watching this whole thing, remembering all the arguments they'd had over the last three and a half years.

If Jesus hadn't intervened, I think they would have cornered the sons of Zebedee and said, "Now guys, we've fought over this issue a lot over the last few months, but to get your own mother and have her bow down to Jesus!

That's a low blow. We've seen how Jesus reacts when people come to worship Him and bow and wash His feet, but we never thought you had it so bad that you would bring your own mother to bow down and worship Him so you could get lead positions among us. So you think you deserve to get second and third place beside His throne, do you?"

I think I know what they were mad about: They didn't think of it first! Deep inside, every one of these twelve men had a secret desire to be elevated, to be promoted, to be exalted, to be recognized, and to be applauded. They had just listened to someone else say what they had been dreaming about for more than three years! Now they had created a very hostile environment. Ten men watched a woman bow down and they became angry and indignant, and maybe just a little envious. They probably sat there secretly thinking, This looks like a master stroke of genius. Maybe it would have been a "master stroke" with anyone else but the Master.

Jesus perceived a wonderful opportunity to try to teach them one more time about something that they knew nothing about: Servanthood.

> But Jesus called them unto him, and said, Ye know that the princes of the Gentiles exercise dominion over them, and they that are great exercise authority upon them.
>
> But it shall not be so among you: but whosoever will be great among you, let him be your minister;
>
> And whosoever will be chief among you, let him be your servant.
>
> **Matthew 20:25-27**

The disciples were operating under the world's idea of advancement and success. It hasn't changed a bit over the centuries either: The world believes that the more people you have under you, the more people you can manipulate, the more people you can dominate, the more people you can command, and the more people you control with money, then the greater you are. That is the world's concept of greatness (and you can include most of us in that batch too!).

There's probably not a parent reading these words who would not be hurt if their son or daughter just worked at a menial job the rest of their life, especially if you have done your best to get him or her in some profession or a special training program so they "can be somebody."

Jesus wants to lift us higher into God's realm. He says, "This is how the world views greatness. And it is not so among you. For the way it works in My Father's kingdom is this: Whoever wishes to be great among you shall be your servant." (See Matthew 20:26.)

Have you ever heard anyone proudly stand up or raise their hand to say, "When I grow up, I don't want to be great. I want to be a nobody." Have you ever heard an adult in their right mind say, "I don't want anybody to know I was ever here. I don't want to ever make a mark; I don't want to achieve anything. I don't want to accomplish anything. I want to be a nobody!"

If we look at the way the members of our churches live today, we might think we all want to slip through life and accomplish nothing, leave no mark, and die a nobody! Most of us are content to put in our hours in the services, drop some cash in the plate now and then, and get on with our "real life."

Those believers who have a "church background," may have been taught in childhood that "if you are ever going to be something, you have to be humble." Now that key word "humble" could mean anything from pushing your car to church (that used to rank you just below sainthood) to wearing your "holey-est" pair of pants and shoes to church on Sundays. This can really confuse the issue of leadership

142

and servanthood in God's kingdom. We used to sing songs on Sunday that told us over and over, "...for such a worm as I." I'll be honest with you — I had great difficulty seeing myself as a worm crawling in the mud and dirt of life. Who wants to be a worm? We talked more about being a sinner than about being a saint in those days — it was more "humble" to show how rotten you were before you were saved. A person could get in trouble for having "high and mighty" ideas about ministry or accomplishment.

True humility is still rare in the Church today. Most of what passes for humility isn't genuine. Before we snub our noses at the old days of false humility, we need to take a close look at the modern brands of false humility. How many of you have heard "humble" testimonies like this?

"I want to testify, Pastor. You know the other day, I went to the hospital to pray for one of our members, and when I went into that hospital room and laid my hands on that man, why the burning power of the Holy Ghost just rushed through my body. That Holy Ghost power hit that man like a bolt of lightning from my hand, and the power of the Holy Ghost brought him up when I obeyed God and laid my hand on him. God began to heal him...but just give God the glory."

If God used you to heal someone of AIDS, what would you do? Many Christians would know exactly what they would do. First, they would want to write a book, and then they would get themselves on the Christian television and radio shows, because they "just have to give God the glory" for what He did through them. Jesus is the only man I know Who constantly healed people and didn't tell anybody.

This twisted concept of humility is one of our problems. Jesus was truly humble, but when people would come up to Him and ask, "Who do you think You are?" He would answer matter-of-factly, "I am the Son of God." True humility does not mean we have to act stupid. It is declaring who and what you are by the grace of God, with no additions and no subtractions. It has nothing to do with you — you are who you are by God's grace.

Jesus was direct and to the point with the disciples. His time was near, and He had to drive home this truth if these hard cases were to survive what would come in the next few days. When I see Jesus talking to the eleven men who would lead the first Church on earth (and Judas the betrayer), I hear it this way:

"Sons of Zebedee, this contending for chief positions is the world's way. Don't snicker, Peter...each of you has thought the same thing in your hearts. Now hear God's way: Whoever wishes to be great can have it. It is not just for a few super-spiritual giants in God. Whoever wishes to be great — whether you are rich or poor, educated or ignorant — whether you are black, white or polka-dot — I don't even care if you are male or female — whoever wishes to be great...must become the servant of all." (From Matthew 20:25-27.)

Do you realize that one of the basic problems with our youth today is that traditional Christianity offers them nothing but the grand opportunity to be a worm in life. They are attracted to the world because God put a dream of greatness in their hearts that the Church is trying to kill. We offer them a dream of worms in the dirt; the world tells them to dream about becoming a rock star, rolling in money. Teenagers dream about being somebody, because it hasn't been beaten out of them yet by the Church system or by society.

There is room in the kingdom of God for greatness, but everyone in God's kingdom must wear a servant's towel to work. Anyone who wants greatness can have it. The problem is that God's idea of greatness is just a little bit different than ours. It is contrary to every nerve and fiber of our being.

Look closely at the Lord's words in Matthew 20:26, **...but whosoever will be great among you....** *The New American Standard* version says, **...whoever wishes to become great among you....** Christians don't understand that greatness is already in us. The potential or the seed is planted in us at birth by God. We become great, we don't just do great things. Most of us want to do great things for God, but God is not as interested in the doing as He is in the being.

"Greatness" in God's eyes comes through our becoming, not just through our doing. The only way you and I can become great is to go to the school of the Holy Spirit, to pay the price and drink the cup of the Lord. This strips away those things hiding the greatness God planted within us. You see, God is not just doing great things, God in and of Himself is Great!

Most of us think of "great ministries" when we think of greatness in God's kingdom. We think of astounding miracles and signs and wonders. We think of huge crowds and crowded altars, and empty wheelchairs and anointed musicians who can sway a crowd with their music.

We think of great acts; God thinks of great character. We remember the image of men in the height of their charisma; God remembers seeing His own image in the life of a submitted servant who faithfully fulfills his destiny in God with joy.

Throughout the New Testament, God emphasizes our responsibility to bear fruit. The fruit of the Spirit deals with God's nature, character and personality in us! He wants us to manifest His greatness in our mortal bodies. The only way we can achieve greatness and bear the fruit of His character is to die for it. None of us has ever learned to value the Spirit like God does. You want to pack out a church, get someone who can move in the gifts, signs, and wonders. And yes, we do want to see these things in the

Church. But these dramatic manifestations will draw a crowd even if the minister doesn't have much in the Christ-like character column.

God delights to get a man who just loves Him with all his heart. He'll take that man who has paid the price to gain godly integrity and character, and He'll build His Church with that man. Twenty years from now, that church will still be together and growing, fulfilling its destiny in God without strife or instability. As the shepherd goes, so goes the flock.

Every man or woman who has ever felt called to full-time ministry, or prayed, "God, I want to be great, I want a great and powerful ministry. I want to be great in Your kingdom," has heard the voice of Jesus say, "Become a servant." Some of us — maybe all of us — said, "No, no, no. You don't understand, God. I want to be great." In any case, the answer is always the same. Jesus told the disciples and He tells us today, **...whosoever will be great among you, let him be your minister** (Matthew 20:26).

You and I are each called to be a servant for the Lord. Say the word *servant* several times out loud:

Servant. Servant. Servant.

This word ties into your purpose and destiny. Whoever wishes to be great among you, must become your servant. Don't be deceived at this point either: There is a vast difference between servant-like actions and true servanthood. I have grown up in the church all my life, and I have watched people do servant-like things. I've seen people who cook all the food in the church. I've seen others who clean the building, and paint and do a lot of other servant-like things. I found out early in life that doing these kinds of things doesn't make someone a servant.

You can do servant-like things, but that will never make you a servant. "Whoever wishes to become great must become your servant." Jesus knows our thoughts. He kept going beyond His first point and seemingly insults us, **And whosoever will be chief** [or first] **among you, let him be your servant** (Matthew 20:27).

"Oh, my God, that's what I want to be! I want to be first. I want to be Numero Uno." Jesus says, **Whoever wishes to be first among you shall be your slave** (Matthew 20:27 NASB).

How many times have you seen the terms *slave, bondslave, servant,* or *prisoner* in the apostolic epistles of James, Peter, John and Paul? After a while, you cannot help but notice that there comes a point when they pen the words, "I, the servant of the Lord Jesus...." That seems to be a more important "credential" or title than, "I, the apostle." Sometimes, they took it a step further and wrote, "I, the bondslave of Jesus." Then Paul would take it out of all comprehension and write, "I, the prisoner of the Lord." These men understood that the height of spiritual maturity was reached only in the place of greatness, when a man or woman reflected the very image, nature and character of God in the earth.

The only way to become great is to become a servant. You can do all the servant-like things you want —you can paint the nursery walls, lay the carpet, cook food for the hungry and homeless, you can visit the sick, and you can take groceries to people. All of these good deeds are wonderful, but they will not make you a servant. Whoever wishes to be great must become a servant. God is a great God because He is great by nature. He can't change what He is, which is a servant.

God is a servant by nature. No matter what you do, no matter how far you go away from God, it is God's nature to rule you, to pour out to you, to come to you, and to love you. It doesn't matter if you think you have earned it (you haven't), or if you think you are worthy of it (you aren't, and neither am I). It doesn't matter if you deserve it (you don't, but who does?). God by nature is great because God is a servant.

There is a second dimension to leadership and the towel of servanthood that Jesus modeled for us perfectly. More than nearly any other subject, this topic relates directly to destiny and God's purposes.

I can imagine Jesus when He was about 12 years of age, playing with His friends. I can see them as they stopped for a moment to have one of those "deep discussions" about life that kids have so often. One of the little guys said to another, "When you grow up, what are you going to become?" "When I grow up, I think I'm going to become a leader of the Sadducees, like Papa." I can see another one lean over and poke the future Sadducee in the side and brag, "Well that's nothing! When I grow up, I'm going to be a Pharisee and be on the Sanhedrin, like Gamaliel." I can even hear one smart-aleck from the tribe of Levi say, "When I grow up, I'm going to become the high priest of all Israel."

Finally, I can just imagine the scene when someone looks at Jesus and says, "Jesus, what are You going to be when You grow up?" "When I grow up, I'm going to be the greatest servant of all." "No, no, no, Jesus, you don't understand. We're not talking about now. We know that You have to obey Your Father and Your Mother, and the rabbis at the synagogue. But when You grow up and You don't have to come under them, what are You going to be?" I can see Him stand up and say, "I'm going to be the Passover Lamb — I'm going to give My life."

At the age of twelve, Jesus understood His destiny. I can imagine Him respectfully telling His earthly mother and father, "Why are you looking for Me? Didn't you know where I would be? I am not concerned about My business. I'm not occupied with My concerns, or desires. I must be about My Father's business if I am to be the greatest of servants! I am absorbed and single-minded about doing My father's business. My very meat and drink is to do His will. I don't live by natural food, but by every word that comes out of His mouth. This is not My will, but His." (See Luke 2:41-52.)

Nowhere is this principle of leadership by submission more powerfully demonstrated than in the 13th chapter of the gospel of John.

Now before the feast of the passover, when Jesus knew that his hour was come that he should depart out of this world unto the Father, having loved his own which were in the world, he loved them unto the end.

And supper being ended, the devil having now put into the heart of Judas Iscariot, Simon's son, to betray him;

Jesus knowing that the Father had given all things into his hands, and that he was come from God, and went to God;

He riseth from supper, and laid aside his garments; and took a towel, and girded himself.

After that he poureth water into a basin, and began to wash the disciples' feet, and to wipe them with the towel wherewith he was girded.

Then cometh he to Simon Peter: and Peter saith unto him, Lord, dost thou wash my feet?

Jesus answered and said unto him, What I do thou knowest not now; but thou shalt know hereafter.

Peter saith unto him, Thou shalt never wash my feet. Jesus answered him, If I wash thee not, thou hast no part with me.

Simon Peter saith unto him, Lord, not my feet only, but also my hands and my head.

Jesus saith to him, He that is washed needeth not save to wash his feet, but is clean every whit: and ye are clean, but not all.

For he knew who should betray him; therefore said he, Ye are not all clean.

So after he had washed their feet, and had taken his garments, and was set down again, he said unto them, Know ye what I have done to you?

Ye call me Master and Lord: and ye say well; for [so] I am.

If I then, your Lord and Master, have washed your feet; ye also ought to wash one another's feet.

For I have given you an example, that ye should do as I have done to you.

Verily, verily, I say unto you, The servant is not greater than his lord; neither he that is sent greater than He that sent him.

If ye know these things, happy are ye if ye do them.

I speak not of you all: I know whom I have chosen: but that the scripture may be fulfilled, He that eateth bread with me hath lifted up his heel against me.

Now I tell you before it come, that, when it is come to pass, ye may believe that I am he.

Verily, verily, I say unto you, He that receiveth whomsoever I send receiveth Me; and he that receiveth me receiveth him that sent me.

When Jesus had thus said, he was troubled in spirit, and testified, and said, Verily, verily, I say unto you, that one of you shall betray me.

John 13:1-21

Jesus always knew the timing of God. He always perceived the hour, the season, and even the minutes of what He was to do on the earth. There were times in His ministry when men would try to kill Him, and He would stop them cold with statements like, "What's wrong with you? It's not My time to die." Men from His own hometown tried to throw Him over a cliff, and others tried to stone Him. He just moved them aside and walked away...it wasn't His time to die.

The Son of God, Who had never been severed or separated from the Father, lived in continual peace, regardless of His surroundings. We never find Jesus living in fear, stress, anxiety or depression. He just flowed within His Father's purposes. On the other hand, I have discovered that when something is trying to move one way, and another thing stops it, we call that resistance. Many times in my life I have felt tremendous pressure because my will was in conflict with God's will. God's affections began to press against my affections. His desires began to press against my desires. Jesus didn't live that way (and I shouldn't). There was no pressure or resistance in Jesus' life, because Jesus' will was the Father's. Any outside pressure was meaningless to Him because He lived within the perfect will and provision of the Father.

One version of the gospel says that Jesus set His face like flint toward Jerusalem, knowing He was the Lamb of God going to His death. Yet there was no pressure, no strife, no anxiety, and no fear. Jesus just flowed in the will of the Father. But He knew that He had twelve men who loved Him, and He loved them. The success of everything He had done over the last three years and more was going to depend on those twelve men. The Bible says that He loved them to the end (John 13:1), and He knew that He was going to Jerusalem to spend His last hours with them in the Upper Room.

What would He say to them? What had they failed to learn in the last three years that He must again plant in their minds? A picture is worth a thousand words we are told. What picture did He paint that made such an impression on them that years later, when they taught new believers and recalled their training with Him, the picture He painted would bring total recall of every word He spoke and every deed He did in their company?

I believe that as our Savior walked slowly toward His destiny in Jerusalem, He was giving careful thought and purpose to everything He would say to these men. He was going to paint the grand finale.

In verse two, Jesus and the disciples were all in the Upper Room, and they had just finished their Passover meal. The devil had already put it into the heart of Judas Iscariot, Simon's son, to betray Jesus.

Verse 3 reveals one of the great keys to effective ministry in the life of Jesus Christ.

> **Jesus knowing that the Father had given all things into his hands, and that he was come from God, and went to God.**
>
> John 13:3

Whenever God gives you something in life, there will came a time when He will say, "Put it back on the altar." Even Jesus Christ, Who had come from God, had to go back to God. If God ever gives you a house, there will come a time when God will say, "Lay it on the altar." If God gives you a mate, He will say, "Lay your love on the altar." When God gives you a job or a blessing, lay it on the altar. Whenever God blesses you, there's a time when he will test you like Abraham and say, "Lay it on the altar."

> **He [Jesus] riseth from supper, and laid aside his garments; and took a towel, and girded himself.**
>
> John 13:4

Jesus suddenly stood up and began taking His clothes off to His skivvies and took a towel and wrapped it around Himself. Incidentally, this is not a Jewish custom. Jesus was shocking everybody. (Now if you don't believe me, then eat dinner one night at a local restaurant and, at an assigned time, just stand up and start to take your clothes off. I promise you, you will have everybody's attention — no matter how "average" you look. Even the people who are asleep will wake up!)

What was Jesus doing? He was painting the picture, the grand finale of something He wanted to put in their heads.

They would never forget it. As they were finishing the meal, He stood up silently, took His clothes off and wrapped Himself with a towel. You see, Jesus had tested every one of these men that very night.

When the men entered the room, everything was there when they got there. The table was set. The food was ready. Everything was in place — except for one thing. According to Jewish custom and tradition, when you entered any house, business or establishment, there were to be three important items right inside of the door: a water pitcher full of water, a water basin, and a towel. The servant of that house (if you were rich enough to own one), was to wash the dirt off your feet. It was a Jewish tradition. If the household couldn't afford servants, then the person who was "the lowest on the totem pole" was expected to wash everyone else's feet.

But that particular day, the room was ready, and the disciples — the evangelist's staff and ministry support team — started walking in. Peter walked in, but he didn't see any servants around. He glanced back toward the door and saw those three items laid side by side, and he thought to himself, "That's not for me. Maybe the sons of Thunder, Mr. Two and Mr. Three would like to try their hand at it." James walked in, "That's not for me." His brother John walked in with a strut, and noticed the two ahead of him already sitting down and the absence of a servant. He thought, "Looks like one of us is going to be blessed with a dirty job, but hey, I'm a son of Thunder. It's not for me." He sat down as close to the head of the table as possible. One by one, each of the twelve walked in, glanced back at the door, and quickly settled into a place at the table. Not one of them assumed the duties of the custom. They didn't know it, but they had just failed a crucial test of their discipleship.

Jesus purposely walked in, ignoring the three items at the door, and took His place at the head of the table. He specifically dismissed the servants after the table had been set. Now, He stood up and said, "For three and a half years, every one of you men have missed it. You have fought and argued over who is to be the greatest in the kingdom. But none of you has understood the true path to greatness. None of you has developed the heart of a servant."

Then the King of all kings, the Lord of lords, God in the flesh stripped off His outer garments, wrapped Himself with a towel, the symbol of servitude, and began to wash the dirt off their feet with His own hands. The Lord of the Universe was washing off more than dirt from the dusty roads of Israel — He was washing away their foolish pride and envy. He was destroying with every drop of water their preconceived ideas about greatness and godliness. Lifetimes of tradition and misguided thinking were carried away in that basin of dirty water that day.

How did God's chosen King choose to have His kingship remembered and marked throughout the generations of man? His symbol of kingship is not a crown. It is not a sword. It is not a scepter. If you want to understand what makes Jesus King of kings and Lord of lords on planet earth, then look at His hand-picked symbol of His authority — He took the servant's towel.

As God in flesh knelt down and began to wash the dirt off their feet, He told the disciples, "You have missed it, John. James, do you understand why I do what I do? I too wish to be great in My Father's kingdom, but I desire it for His glory. And I have understood the path to greatness. From my youth, Nathaniel, I have paid the price, not only to be great, but to be first. I am the willing slave of My Father God."

Jesus burned a simple message in the hearts of His disciples that night: If you want to be great in the kingdom of God, learn to deal in dirt. Jesus was great in God's kingdom, not only because He was God's Son, but also because Jesus fulfilled His Father's desire by serving Him with a servant's heart. He simply was what He was destined to be. Everywhere He went, people were attracted to Him. These weren't just "good people" either. He met and ministered to adulterers, harlots, thieves, lepers, and tax gatherers. Sinners and total outcasts were attracted to Him wherever He went.

He drew them like a magnet. Yet somehow, when Jesus was in their midst, He never left them the same. He came in with His servant's towel, and He left with the dirt of their sin. Many times they brought Him the sick by the hundreds. One time, the crowd was so large and packed that two men carrying a paralyzed friend on a litter couldn't even get to the door of the house where Jesus was. Desperate, and filled with a strange boldness, the men somehow boosted the litter to the roof, and then they tore a hole in the roof and lowered their paraplegic friend right into the room before Jesus. Jesus saw him, and showed no surprise at the way he had arrived. Everyone there thought they knew what the man wanted and needed. He needed to be healed.

Once again, Jesus the Servant would follow another command from a Higher Authority. "You are going to see greatness. You are going to see God in the flesh." Then He looked at the man and said, "Thy sins are forgiven." The religious men in the room got angry — they had never counted on this kind of heresy from this rabbi! "Who does He think He is to forgive sin?" (See Luke 5:18-26.)

Jesus knew their thoughts, and His Father had ordained this event to provide yet another proof to the world that Jesus was the Son of God. "Which is easier to say, thy sins be forgiven or rise and walk?" One of the greatest things God has taught me as a leader is that I can call people down to receive Christ day after day, because He has given me authority. And I have the authority (just like you do as a minister of reconciliation) to look them in the eye and I say, "God told me to tell you this — your sins are forgiven."

We don't understand the power that God has given us. We don't understand the path of greatness. True greatness was demonstrated in the flesh in that Upper Room, only days away from the most tragic death in human history, followed by the birth of the Church. The Bible says that Satan had already entered Judas when Jesus Christ rose to take up the servant's towel. At one point that night, God in the flesh knelt down before Satan in the flesh, with the servant's towel in His hand, and the impossible happened. God the Father, through the Son, looked at Satan the fallen servant angel indwelling Judas, and said, "I will wash the dirt off your feet. I forgive you, but I will never condone your rebellion. This is why I Am that I Am — the Great One, and why you, little created one, are not."

Our churches don't teach greatness. Scripture says, **You which are spiritual, restore...** (Galatians 6:1). If you really want to test how spiritual you are, don't measure it by your preaching ability, or by how many people are healed when you pray for them. Ask yourself, "How many people have I helped to restore in the last year? How many people have I really forgiven recently?"

Nothing has hurt me more in the last ten years than to watch major leaders in the Church of Jesus Christ fall into sin. And I've hurt even more as I looked for the generals, the leaders of the Church to come forward to restore the fallen. Where are the spiritual among us? Where is our spirituality? Where is our greatness? Many pastors and Church leaders across America live in a special kind of fear because they know the American church world isn't known for its ability to forgive and restore. Fear causes them to live in an unrealistic world where they don't dare make a mistake. And if they are dealing with a difficult temptation, they don't dare share it with anyone, because it will be in the newspaper before they can hang up the phone. Where can these men and women in leadership go for ministry in this land? Where can they go for healing? Where can they touch the greatness of God?

The problem we have all faced in the Church is that we can usually find someone who is willing to try to wash the dirt off, but they don't know when to stop! They won't stop with the dirt, they will take off the skin! That is why we come away from a "cleansing" with needless wounds and scars. This happens because there is very little greatness in the Church of Jesus Christ. It is time for us to once again recall the picture of our Lord kneeling at our feet with a servant's towel on His arm and a basin of cleansing water in His nail-scarred hands.

God is not looking for super-stars. He is looking for servants. When He looks for leaders, He looks for the greatest servants among us — those with a servant's attitude in their heart and a serving towel over their arm. He is searching for people who will drink the cup and pay the price to become servants in their nature. I was a janitor at our church for five years, and I can honestly tell you that I never developed a nature of servanthood. All it did was break my spirit. When I finally discovered the heart of servanthood, my whole life changed, because I had become the friend of God. You can never become a friend of God until you first become a servant of God.

Abraham became the friend of God because he became God's servant. When I think of power, I think of people like Moses, who commanded the Red Sea to split, and turned the Nile River into blood. But when Moses died, God said He would personally write his epitaph. What did God say about Moses? God didn't recount all the great things Moses had done, He simply said, **Moses my servant is dead** (Joshua 1:2). That was the highest compliment God could pay His friend and servant.

I have been walking with God since the age of eight, and I know that I have not yet achieved the level of servanthood where I could write in a book, "I, the bondslave" or "I, the prisoner." But I have a deep desire to hear my Master say when I stand before Him, "Well done, My good and faithful servant. Enter into My rest."

About the Author

Don Meares has traveled extensively preaching the gospel on five continents. He is widely sought for his insight on corporate destiny and church structure. He is regarded as having an apostolic-prophetic ministry to the Church at large. On a local church level, he is Senior Pastor of Evangel Church, a multi-racial congregation of several thousand in suburban Washington, DC.